Home from the Hill

Home from the Hill

R. W. F. Poole

Illustrations by Reginald Bass

MICHAEL JOSEPH
LONDON

MICHAEL JOSEPH LTD

Published by the Penguin Group
27 Wrights Lane, London W8 5TZ, England
Viking Penguin Inc., 375 Hudson Street, New York, New York 10014, USA
Penguin Books Australia Ltd, Ringwood, Victoria, Australia
Penguin Books Canada Ltd, 10 Alcorn Avenue, Toronto, Ontario, Canada M4V 3B2
Penguin Books (NZ) Ltd, 182–190 Wairau Road, Auckland 10, New Zealand

Penguin Books Ltd, Registered Offices: Harmondsworth, Middlesex, England

First published in Great Britain 1997
1 3 5 7 9 10 8 6 4 2

Set in 10.5/13pt Monotype Plantin Light
Typeset by Rowland Phototypesetting Ltd, Bury St Edmunds, Suffolk
Printed in England by Clays Ltd, St Ives plc

A CIP catalogue record for this book is available from the British Library

ISBN 0718I 4202 0

The moral right of the authors has been asserted

CONTENTS

INTRODUCTION

In 1987 I started writing a column in the Weekend Section of the *Daily Telegraph*. My remit was to write about my 'life and times in the countryside'. So this is a book of journalistic life and times, being a collection of those pieces written between 1 January 1993 and 31 December 1995. You would think, therefore, that a collection of pieces already written and paid for once would be money for old rope. So it might seem, but Publishers do not buy old rope and are very keen on something that they like to call 'melding and meshing'. This means that some of the articles have been altered slightly for the book, and I hope that you think that they have been properly improved, sanitised, homogenised and, very probably, pasteurised.

As these pieces were written for a daily newspaper on matters that were current at that time, anachronism is inevitable. Some of the people that you will read about have died, retired or have been otherwise translated to other spheres. Whatever, I had a great deal of fun in the researching of the articles and met numerous very nice people, many of whom have become friends. To all those who helped with these pieces, often at some personal inconvenience, I would like to offer my sincere gratitude – without their help there would have been no pieces and no column. This also applies to you, The Reader – without your loyalty and encouragement, the column would no longer exist and I would just be another of the wrecks that litter Fleet Street.

I would also like to thank all the Editors and other kind people in the various parts of the *Telegraph* who have tolerated the strange, bucolic figure who occasionally shambles through the offices at Canary Wharf, usually tripping over things and spilling cups of tea. I would like to thank, particularly, Max Hastings, without whom the column would never have started, and Charles Moore, who has benignly allowed it to continue. Special thanks also to all those at the Weekend Section, past and present, for their help and good humour. Extra special thanks to John Carey, who has 'minded' the column almost from the beginning and has become a great friend and ally. John and I are survivors from the start of the original Weekend Section in 1987. I cannot leave the 'thank yous' without Jenny Dereham, my long-suffering and much admired publisher at Michael Joseph, for whom I have been the cause of executive stress since 1988 – I think that this is our seventh book together.

I thought I should include a political prognosis in this introduction. As this is being written at the time of the May 1997 election, it is hard to say what the state of the Nation will be by the time that you read this – always supposing that we still have a Nation and no one has pawned it in the meantime. However, I can tell you what the unofficial Home Office prognosis is – total political and social breakdown by the year 2050. This suggests that the Home Office shares my opinion of the total lack of ability amongst politicians of all parties. It also seems to share my opinion that once we have been sold into a 'Single Currency' and the Euro bank has its hands on our reserves which will be used to pay all those pensions and social security that our European chums cannot afford, then the whole structure will implode in violence and anarchy.

The cause of all our troubles is quite simple, if you look at it with a stockman's eye – there are too many people and we are keeping them in exactly the sort of unnatural conditions that we complain about for animals. We have become 'Battery Humans' and our behaviour exactly mirrors the vices found amongst intensively kept animals – feather pecking, tail biting and cannibalism – their human equivalents are to be seen everywhere. Nature solves the problem of over-population in its own way – with disease and starvation. The Human Animal adds the dimension of violence.

My prognosis for the traditional country life is dim and grim. Often, in the past, I have compared the plight of the Ab-original countryman in this country to that of the Native Americans in the last century. Indeed, since I became a sort of 'tame Indian' occasionally allowed to wander amongst the 'Chattering Classes', I have come to realise how huge is the culture gap between Us and Them. To Urban Person, the British Countryman might as well be from another world and, of course, it is another world. To Urban Person, we are an inconvenient minority who cling to apparently archaic customs. It is quite obvious (to UP) that we are a barrier to progress. A progress that will see all the English countryside turned into a theme park for Urban Person to frolic in.

Come! Come! I hear you cry – this is not a very cheerful Author's Introduction. You have the right to say that, but then I am not a very cheerful author just at the moment. Since I started writing about the countryside, I have seen the rural traditions and the way of life that I love and believe in being demolished brick by brick, stone by stone. Thus far, country people have shrugged their shoulders and got on with life, but remember G. K. Chesterton's poem The Secret People:

> We hear men speaking for us of new laws strong and sweet,
> Yet is there no man speaketh as we speak in the street . . .
> . . . For we are the people of England, that never have spoken yet.

Believe me, when we do, you will all hear it.

In the meantime, I hope that in this book you may find just a flavour of a way of life that is now threatened with extinction. Taste and enjoy, whilst you can.

R. W. F. Poole

1. ABOUT THE AUTHOR

[1]

I learned to row in the pram. To be more exact, it was a 'prahm', a Baltic-style dinghy whose swept-up bow came to a squared-off end. These handy little craft were much used as boats' tenders in Fowey Harbour. It would be an exaggeration to say that I could row before I could walk, but it sounds good. I cannot remember the time when I could not row. I just grew up with it, in a family of 'blue-nosed' sailor persons and still have a love of boats that has been seldom requited in the last twenty years. I never mastered

Pythagoras but I am one of the few persons now alive who knows the difference between a barquentine and a brigantine and who would know where you should put your lower topgallant.

I learned to row properly; that is 'feathering the blade' (turning it parallel to the surface of the water as the rower comes forward) unlike the harbour men who always kept their blades vertical, as is practised in the Navy, I believe. I also learned to scull. This done with a single oar over the transom making a sort of figure of eight motion, which somehow moves a boat along.

After sailing, when the Cornish crabber was safe at her moorings, it was my duty to row Father back to the boat house. Father would souse his not inconsiderable bulk in the stern sheets. This brought the up-swept bow of the prahm even further out of the water and meant that I was perched nearly vertically as I rowed. ' "Row for the shore, boys," ' said the king, ' "and we shall hear those churchmen sing," ' Father would bellow from the stern as my puny arms tugged on the oars, remembering that 'real sailors don't cry over a little blister'.

Rowing was the normal way of getting about the harbour in those days. Outboard motors were just starting and, usually, stopping. They then had to be rowed home whilst being stripped and reassembled to the accompaniment of much salty language. After re-assembly there was always one bit left over.

Regattas always included rowing races. There were 'Randan' races where there were three men in the boat: a bow oar, a stroke oar and a pair of sculls in the middle. Then there were the 'Gig' races. In the old days, competing pilots would be rowed out to ships in the offing by their gig crews. The winner got the job and the fee. This provoked fierce competition between crews. Pilots now go out by launch, but Gig racing maintains in its full ferocity. Father always brought down a crew from Oxford to row in the Gig race. I always yearned to cheer for Fowey or Polruan, but was told sternly that sportsmen and gentlemen always cheered for the visitors. Not that my cheers ever did them much good. Cornish brawn and raw power inevitably seemed to triumph over the polished skill of golden youth. This always chuffed the locals who reckoned that Fowey and Polruan would 'walk the bliddy boat race'.

Even at home there was no escape from rowing. The walls of the Smoking Room were covered in oars with names painted on them. There were fading photographs of lean young men in impossible scarves, of college fours and college eights and of Father in the Oxford Boat on two successive years with defeat written over his slumped body and face.

There was never any doubt that I would be a 'Wet Bob' (rower) at Eton. Even if there had been, the horrors of cricket at my prep school would have strengthened my resolve: that nasty hard ball which hurt the hand and made people shout at you when you very properly dropped it, and what on earth was a 'box' for?

Alf, the Head Boatman at Rafts (the Eton Boat House) and a man with a truly amazing memory, remembered Father: 'You'll be looking to get in the Eight,' he said, 'if you're as good as your dad.' Ah! the dreams of youth.

Such dreams were hard to maintain in a 'whiff'. A whiff is the basic sculling boat, solid and clinker-built with a fixed seat. It was designed to be idiot-proof, but sometimes had its work cut out. It was also the lowest form of life on the river and got shouted and megaphoned at by everybody. '*Ahead Whiff!*' would bellow the lordly eight sweeping up astern, causing complete panic in the whiff's timorous breast and frantic evasive action straight into the path of a house four sweeping downstream and 'giving her ten' (full ahead): '*Ahead Whiff!! STOPPERALL!!!*' (emergency stop) bringing the trembling whiff under close scrutiny from four hot and angry young men and the extreme disdain that all coxes cultivate to compensate for being vertically challenged.

From a whiff I graduated to a 'rigger'. This is the generally recognised sculling boat, with a smooth skin and a sliding seat: a true transport of delight. The rigger allowed me to explore miles upstream beyond Boveney Locks, to savour the glutinous river smells, the wafting essence of new-mown hay and to study the life of the river banks, which included guardsmen doing fascinating things to ladies of the town.

But what of my ambitions for the Eight, an Oxford Blue and inheriting Father's little Leander cap and pink socks? I laboured in Pairs and Fours and Lower Eights. I lusted after powder-blue socks (Eight only) in Messrs New & Lingwood's shop window. Somehow I failed to achieve early promise. It might just have been that I totally lacked team and competitive spirit. It might just have been that I had started smoking a pipe and got a taste for beer. It might just have been that I was more inclined to shout '*Up* the school!!' than 'up the *SCHOOL*!!' For whatever reason, I failed even to get my Lower Boats (white cap with concentric strawberry rings). The nearest I ever got to the Eight was twelve of the best from the strong arm of the Captain of Boats for being 'a thorough bloody nuisance'. After that I gave up rowing and took up beagling instead: made me the man I am today.

[2]

It is unfashionable to wear a hat in London these days. This is a stupid fashion since something like a third of your body heat goes out through your head or, if you are bald and sexy like me, probably more. So all you bare-headed fashionable people have semi-permanent colds and good luck to you. Me, I always wear a hat, a rather battered felt job. All you smart city folk stare at me through your sniffles. In the country, we peasants always wear hats. I favour a good 'ecky thump' tweed cap and so does 'Ard Jock'. In fact you never see Jock without his cap – except when it rains; then he takes it off. We did suggest once that he should keep it on in the rain. He was indignant: 'What! what! and sit arl neet in the hoose in a wet cap!' There is no answer to that.

[3]

I was fascinated to read somewhere that every Oxford College now has two full-time 'Harassment Officers'. Such persons would have a thin time in the country where a bit of honest rutting is regarded as entirely natural. Should some ardent swain stray beyond acceptable limits, then a swift clip round the ear usually solves the problem. Should this not answer then the lady's absolutely enormous mother (she that can carry four hay bales at once and who is thought to chew glass for breakfast) might just drop round for a quiet word. Whatever the problem it is solved in a traditional manner: feminism and sexism seldom rear their tousled heads; rural ladies have no need of them.

A few years ago, a friend and I were stalking on the west coast of Scotland. The resident stalker, whom we will call Jock, was one of those monolithic Highlanders who appeared to be carved out of a 7-foot block of granite. We were all having a dram one evening and the question of political correctness came up. We asked Jock whether he ever had problems with feminism up the glen. His eyes took on a far-away look and he said, 'Aye, aye, whiles we do, but I find that the butt end of a good thick stick is a fine cure.' Well, we slapped our thighs and rocked and rolled with mirth over that one, without ever thinking how utterly appalling our attitudes were.

The size of my 'Negative Attitude Problem' was brought home to me when I spoke recently to a dinner of 'Caring Professionals' and Academics. I have only one speech which has served me well over the years and which contains a number of pretty and wholesome rural anecdotes. It has two versions – all male and mixed. On this occasion, I used the Bowdlerised version. Even so, it did not go well. As I spoke, I could feel the ice of disapproval beginning to seep through the welts of my tackety boots. I was definitely laying an egg.

When I told the story of Jock (as above) it was greeted with what I can only call stunned silence. I suspect that the collective opinion of the company was neatly summed up by the flashing-eyed amazon who stormed up to me as I was getting into my car and said that she considered my speech to be 'the biggest load of sexist **** ' that she had ever heard. Oh dear! Oh dear! I fear that there is little hope for unreconstructed peasants like me.

[4]

Rural poetry is not a thing that gets a great airing, probably because those who have written good authentic stuff are not widely known, or are out of fashion. I know that a lot of well-known poets have claimed to have drawn inspiration from the countryside, but very few of them have been proper bred and buttered countrymen. The ghastly Wordsworth is a case in point. I know that he lived in a cottage in the Lake District and consorted with leech gatherers and spent a lot of time 'wandering lonely as a cloud' (I have had to chant that load of rubbish in a childish treble along with the rest of us) but that does not mean that he was a countryman. His feelings were acquired rather than instinctive. For instinctive poetry about the country you have to turn to people who are now disregarded by the many.

John Masefield caught my imagination when I was a child and a battered and well-thumbed copy of his collected poems has come down through the years with me. He was well known for his sea poems ('I must go down to the sea again, to the lonely sea and the sky . . .') and he was able to write convincingly having sailed 'before the mast' in the days of sail, but he was also a countryman. I suspect that very few people now read his great narrative poem 'Reynard the Fox', although many will have read snippets from it (it is very long). Read the whole, if you can find it and, no, I am sorry, but I do not know where you can get it.

The usual response to the question: 'Do you like Kipling?' is 'I don't know, I've never tried it' and there are a lot of people who never have. This is a great shame because he wrote some wonderful stuff. He loved the English countryside and I have always liked a little poem called 'The Land'.

Now for the man whose work I really go for: William Barnes – the Dorset poet. Barnes was a school teacher and a clergyman but he came from yeoman stock. He was brought up mainly by his aunt and uncle who farmed near Sturminster Newton. He wrote poetry in 'plain English', but the poems that I love best are his Dorset dialect poems. His poetry is beautifully constructed and was much admired by many of the major literary figures of the last century; also by Queen Victoria. His work is sometimes funny, sometimes sad, but always evocative of an English way of life that was changing and disappearing under the rigours of the Enclosures Acts and the post-Napoleonic war agricultural slump. I suppose that his best-known poem is 'My Orcha'd in Linden Lea' which was set to music by Vaughan Williams and was much loved by music teachers in my youth. It also happens to neatly encapsulate my own view of life and I often recite it to myself in those maddening small hours when sleep will not come and phantasmagoria of Bank Managers and HMI Taxes swirl about over the bed head.

I must also commend to you 'The Wife A-Lost', one of the most beautiful pieces of simple poetic grief that I know and if you can read it without a lump in your throat and a handy Kleenex, then you are a stronger person than I.

As far as I know, Barnes is still in print. I wish someone would record some of his poems (properly, not in BBC Mummerset).

[5]

I have a certain coat which I treat as an old friend. It is part of an old stalking suit. It is tattered and torn and patched and darned. It has many pockets. It smells of dogs and whisky and tobacco

7

and all sorts of other things that you would not like to hear about. Most women would not allow it through their door (but then the same could be, and is, said about me), especially as it is made of a tweed that would deafen half the street, but put it amongst the heather and the bracken and it makes me into the invisible man.

2. FRIENDS, FOES AND
FANCY BITS

[1]

One of the things that I have always enjoyed about Ireland is those little shops where you can go in and buy a postage stamp, order half a pound of bacon and, whilst it is being sliced, lean against the counter with a glass of Tullaghmore Dew in your fist. Such civilised shopping has not been available to us Saxons; not until now that is.

The village of Ireby (pop: low hundreds) lies in the rural folds of north-west Cumberland and its vital organs were decaying.

The village shop closed twelve years since. The Black Lion had been empty for over three years. In January 1994 the Post Office was going to close for good and all. A sadly typical story of rural decline.

Paddy McCreanor is a mild and pleasant man with rosy cheeks and a wuffly blond moustache. He lives with his partner Jannicke just outside Ireby. He makes really wonderful videos about country matters. Paddy was depressed about the decline of Ireby and he decided to do something about it. So he bought the Black Lion. He then set about to transform it into Paddy's Bar where you buy your groceries, get your pension and then relax with a glass of something nourishing: grand opening set for 11 December.

This involved the total structural gralloch of the original building in quick time. When the licensing magistrates made their inspection on 9 December, the windows were not in and the paint was still wet. On the Saturday, the pub was ready, the shop was almost ready and the Post Office cannot open until the existing one finally closes.

The bar was amazing. Paddy once designed film sets and had given his flair its head. The walls were oak panelled (ex various defunct churches); where there was wallpaper it had been varnished so that it looked as though it had been distressed by thousands of ounces of shag tobacco; the roof beams were old ship's timbers on which the adze marks were clearly visible; the splendid Victorian pillars on the bar were old table legs and there was a huge open fire. The atmosphere created a feeling of warmth, cosiness and good cheer. This was helped by Arthur, the manager, who immediately thrust a glass of Black Bush into my hand (how did he know?).

Access to the shop was either through the bar or direct from the street. The conjunction will mean that the shop will be open for as long as the pub is open and will be very convenient for the evening. What woman can complain about a man who asks: 'Anything you want from the shop, dear?'

The Grand Opening was scheduled for midday and was to be performed by a celebrity: Sarah-Jane Hall, Ireby's oldest inhabitant. She 'came for a week and stayed seventy-nine years'. The bar was quite full by midday, but we were all shooed out into the street and a coloured ribbon put across the steps for Mrs Hall to cut. 'Pub's been closed for three and half years and I hope that it won't be closed again,' she said. We all cheered and nipped back in for a warmer; it was a bitter day outside and the bitter pump inside was being 'reet soughty' (not working properly). Then it was outside again to watch the Belfagen Women Morris Dancers. They were utterly splendid; a female version of the Cloggies.

That evening, the bar was one solid mass of sweating humanity, men in boiler suits congealing with women straight from a glossy 'country wear' advert. There is always a way round and thus it was that Barry, Dick, Roddy, Martin, Lal (little) John and I gathered in the shop where we could observe the bar and where we could get drinks from Fraser (Paddy's long-suffering assistant) without pushing through the crowd. The bar staff was flat out. Jannicke was pressed into service. Paddy had problems with the till.

'Get us some wine out of the back, lads,' shouted Arthur.

'The Boddingtons is down,' bellowed Fraser. They were shouting because the decibel level was going off the scale and common sense was sliding down it. Snippets of shouted conversation wafted through:

'Man, I'm fit enough to bull cows uphill.'

'Halsatian foxes! like Halsatians.'

'Noo, tha knows me; I wouldn't be a leear (liar) for sake of yan craw (one crow)!'

'Yon feller's all bull, arse and brackins (brackens).'

As is usually the case in Cumberland the hunting songs began. And so it went until it was time to 'gar yam'. As I weaved my way down the village street, I thought what a wonderful idea Paddy's shar, bop and ost poffice was.

'Why don't more villages do the same?' I asked the friendly lamp post that I was clinging to. The lamp post did not know.

★

[2]

Pleasure does not figure largely in my life, the path of a Peasant/Scribbler being a particularly rocky one. One of the few indulgences that I do allow myself is the purchase of glossy magazines about the countryside so that I can read what is going on there. I mean, I only *live* there, which is not the same thing at all. One of the spin-off pleasures from the magazines is the property section. I like to get the after-breakfast pipe going well and play Pick-the-Stately-Estate. Most of all I like to play the Deer Forest game.

I am very fond of stalking and, on occasion, I think how nice it would be to have my own forest. Then common sense taps me on the shoulder and points out that no deer forest has ever been anything but a bottomless fiscal peat hole into which Sassenach proprietors are expected to shovel cartloads of money to show that they are sorry for Culloden. Then there is the West Highland weather which can only be made bearable by a liver-shrivelling intake of whisky, and when it is not raining, the midges come out. It is a strange thing that the Highland Tourist Board literature never mentions the Highland Midge.

Anyway, leafing through my Glossy the other morning, I was interested to see that the Strathvaich Estate was up for sale. I have never been there, but I had just read a fascinating book about it – *Memories of Strathvaich* by Kenneth MacLennan. Mr MacLennan spent most of his life as a stalker on the estate, as his father had been before him. It is a wonderful picture of Highland life and of how important the stalking is as a part of the local economy.

One of the things that really took my fancy was the Strathvaich communication system. You must remember that this was evolved in the days before VHF radios. Suppose that the stalker is high on the face of Craig Dhu (every deer forest has a Craig Dhu), sees the ghillie far below him and wants to know if the chap can see deer – so he lies down and lifts a leg in the air. The ghillie, seeing this, stands up and holds his hands above his head for stags, rubs his ears for hinds or, if he can see no deer at all, waves his hands up and down. There were other signals and it seems that the system worked well for many years. I was glad to hear this because I do remember a somewhat similar system being developed some years ago by an enthusiastic young Master of Foxhounds so that he could communicate with his staff at a distance. It may be that the foxhunting system was more complicated than the stalking one and it may be that the Hunt Staff were not as taken with the idea (or, indeed, the young Master) as they might have been. I do remember standing next to the Whipper-in whilst the young MFH was doing some convoluted semaphoring on some distant hill.

'What on earth does he want now, Bert?' I said.

'Wants his nappy changing,' was Bert's gloomy reply.

[3]

NOTE I visited Monty Roberts in 1994. Since then he has become a household name in the equine world. His book, *The Man Who Talks To Horses*, has become an international bestseller. All HM the Queen's horses and those of the Household Cavalry use 'Join Up' as part of their basic training.

Monty Roberts is quite simply one of the most Extra-Ordinary men that I have ever met: extraordinary cook, extraordinary house designer, extraordinary tree planter. But, perhaps most of all, extraordinary horse trainer whose methods are now used all over the world and not least by Her Majesty the Queen and the Household Cavalry. It was from this august body I first heard of him.

Before we go into more detail, let us look at the man. He is a large quiet man in his middle fifties. He gives an immediate impression of physical and mental power and if he did ever get angry then I would be heading for the tall timber in leaps and bounds.

He is part Cherokee on both sides of his head and comes from a line of horsemen. He has spent all his life working with horses. He was riding in front of his mother's saddle at eleven months and was doing film stunt work at the age of four. Those of you who thrilled to Elizabeth Taylor's equine expertise in *National Velvet* were actually thrilling to Monty in a wig. His parents had a riding school near Salinas in California. His father was a very hard man to his children, an American Indian tradition. There were no soft edges to the young Roberts's upbringing. At the age of eleven he was mucking out twenty-two stalls and schooling six horses before school and straight back into the stable afterwards.

In 1947 he started breaking wild mustangs. 'Breaking' horses then meant just that. The horse's will was broken by physical subjugation. This often had appalling physical and mental results for the horse and could be extremely dangerous for the man. Monty felt that there had to be a better way. He did some work for a rancher named Bill Dorrance, a 'thoughtful and intelligent horseman'. Bill introduced him to the principles of 'Advance and Retreat' which became the essence of the Roberts method. This was based on an old Indian method of hunting deer. Monty had already heard about this method from his Uncle Ray who had been brought up with the Cherokees. If you are on foot with a fairly primitive bow and arrow, then you have to get within forty feet of a deer to kill it. You may take my word for it that this is not easy. The Indians applied psychology to the problem. The Indian hunter would quite simply walk after his prey. He would do this for perhaps a day. When his instincts told him that the time was right, he would turn and walk away. The psychology of the animal is such that it will turn and follow the hunter. Then the hunter would turn and follow the animal again. This yo-yo effect would continue with the distances getting shorter and shorter until the animal was within range. Humans will also respond to 'Advance and Retreat': try it on a person you fancy. I asked Monty if the Indians also used this method for breaking horses? He looked at my wryly and said no, the way the Indians used to break horses was by starving them until they were too weak to resist.

Monty's ideas found no favour with his father or many other people of that time, so in 1951 he set up on his own, training (show horses, jumping horses, and 'cutting' horses), instructing and going on the Rodeo circuit (National Intercollegiate Rodeo Association Team Roping Champion 1956; Bull-Dogging champion 1957). He also decided he needed more education and enrolled at California Poly and achieved a Triple Major (Biology, Agricultural Economics and Animal Science). In his spare time he opened a tack shop and, as if all that was not enough, married his childhood sweetheart and lovely wife of today, Pat. All this was done without any financial assistance; but 'My God, we struggled!' All this time he was working on his method of 'starting' young horses; quite the opposite of 'breaking'.

In 1963 a well-known New York publisher, who admired his work, said that he would set Monty up in a training establishment 'anywhere in the world'. They chose (and chose well) a site in the beautiful and fertile Santa Ynez valley. Monty designed the house, the stables and all the buildings himself and promptly set up a company called Equine Design to do the same for others. He also started 'Insta Tree' based on some ideas that he had formed at university. The trees are grown in nurseries. For replanting they are sprayed twice, then cut off at waist height. The transplant has its butt steeped in 'Ingredient X' (secret, secret) and is then plonked in a hole in the ground, where it grows. In this way people can have instant trees up to 6 inches in diameter and up to 30 feet in height. A lot of people will (and did) say that this is nonsense. Monty claims a 97% success rate and 'we guarantee 'em to live'.

He also loves cooking. He does all the cooking at home (and I will guarantee the results as being delicious) and as a side line he set up an outside catering and Bar-b-q business.

I hope that by now you are getting the flavour of this Extra-Ordinary man, so now let us go and visit him.

*   *   *

It was dark when I arrived at Flag Is Up Farm so there was little to be seen, except a buck and two does (mule deer) on the floodlit lawn. 'Ah good,' said Monty, 'the deer are here.' He opened the window. The does retreated, but the buck came forward to have his head scratched.

The deer are part of the story. When the Robertses first came to the farm, they rarely saw deer although they were certain that they were there. Then one day, Monty saw some coyotes attacking something in the scrub. It was a doe, weak and in poor condition. Monty drove the coyotes off, but knew that they would be back, so he got some wire mesh and built an igloo over the deer who was too weak to move. Each day he put food and water in the igloo and each day she got a little stronger. After three weeks she was strong enough to be released but each day she would return to the same spot where Monty would feed her. She then began to allow the man to walk with her and suddenly he started seeing deer. For the next seventeen years he walked and worked with the deer, learning from them the lessons in animal language and behaviour that he was incorporating into his 'Join Up' method of starting horses. In particular, the deer taught him the interaction between 'flight' animals (such as deer and horses) and 'fight' animals (such as man). The original doe is still alive and is the matriarch of the herd which now numbers c. seventy. We went to look at her the next morning. She came to Monty's whistle whilst several generations grazed around us.

The deer were on the hill behind the farm and from there the whole farm was spread out below us, the horse barns, the railed paddocks, the training track and the beautiful house, all built from scratch in 1966 and now surrounded by the trees that the Robertses had planted. It was a sweep of green lushness in the valley with the mountains making a spectacular backdrop beyond, everything clear and bright in the warm winter sunshine.

There were several horses on the training track, including a nice sort of two-year-old which was trotting quietly round and then stood like an old dolly whilst Monty discussed its progress with the rider. The horse had been at Flag Is Up for fifteen days.

It had been badly treated and had come as a potential killer, having dropped various riders on twelve occasions and put one of them in hospital. We watched as he trotted quietly away. 'There's no horse problems, only people problems.' Monty takes on many of these problem horses. His success has not made him universally popular amongst other trainers. When asked to demonstrate his methods in Argentina, where some of the breaking methods are not ones that you want to hear about, the vested breakers told him to get out or be carried out. Let me describe this method that is so much argued about.

Part of the set up at Flag Is Up is a large, circular covered school with sheer wooden sides, the floor covered in a thick layer of 'tan' (mostly rice husks). Monty stood in the centre with a long lunge rein coiled in his hand. The chestnut colt was brought in: a wild, frightened baby, made aggressive by previous bad handling. The colt had been halter broken which meant that it was accustomed to wearing a head collar and being led about; that was all.

The colt was loosed in the school. Monty immediately started driving it round and round the school by flicking the rein behind it (never hitting it). It was being made to 'go away'. The gentle pressure was kept up and the colt kept going. Then it began to talk. It dropped an ear = 'I'm listening.' Still trotting, it began a licking and chewing motion = 'I'm not aggressive.' Then came the head nodding = 'Look, can't we talk about this?' The pace slowed, but the colt was kept moving. Then it began to look back = 'Please respond to me.' Monty: 'OK, passive.' The colt stopped and turned to face the man. Monty avoided eye contact and turned his back. The colt came up behind him. He turned left and then right. The colt followed at his shoulder. Then he turned to the horse and very gently began to stroke the colt's head; then its back, quarters and belly. The colt stood motionless. All the time Monty was giving a running commentary to his audience. He picked up the near fore foot; then the near hind. He moved to the offside and repeated the process. At this point, a saddle and bridle were brought in and put in the middle of the school. The colt was leery, but followed Monty up to these strange things because he had decided that it was safer to be with Monty than away from him: the 'safety zone'. Monty said that at this stage 95% of horses can be saddled and bridled with their heads free. This colt had come with a dangerous reputation and was in the other 5%, so the lunge rein was clipped to the head collar, but kept loose. The colt stood motionless. First the pad, then the saddle were placed on his back. Calmness was essential: 'If my pulse rate was 100 right now, this colt would be out of here', so soothing words and gentle action were the order of the moment. Very, very, gently the girth was tightened.

Then the colt was driven away again, around the school. Monty kept moving round in the centre, always with his back to the colt. The colt crept up behind him, following his movements like a dog. All of this comes from lessons taught by the deer.

Then came the bridle: the bit was slipped into the mouth and the head piece gradually eased into place. The colt gave a slight start when the reins were slipped over its head. Monty walked away and the colt followed. Still chatting, the man put a pair of long driving reins onto the bridle and, walking behind the horse, began driving it round the school, turning it to left and right, letting it get the feel of the bit. The reins were dropped. The colt stopped and walked back to Monty and its safety area.

In came Richard. Richard Maxwell is an ex-Household Cavalry-man and one of the many who come to learn about Join Up. He was going to do the backing. All those days on the rodeo circuit have caught up with Monty and his own back. Richard walked all around the colt making a fuss of it. Then he was legged up. Initially, he just lay across the saddle, then very slowly put his leg over. Monty began leading the colt around the school. The colt gave one little startled shy; that was all. The lead rein was taken off. The colt walked quietly on. Then trotted. Then was stopped and reined back. Trotted the other way. Stopped and reined back. Richard slipped off his back. That was enough for the first day: 'This is not a normal horse – he's wild, spooky and potentially dangerous.' The colt was quietly led away to his stable. Phew!! total time from start to finish 35 minutes by my watch. Time to reach a similar stage under 'normal breaking methods' – days and perhaps weeks.

Monty's methods are not the norm, although he would like them to be. They are now being used by people he has taught all over the world. He said his big breakthrough was when the Queen asked him to Windsor to demonstrate 'Join Up'. Monty Roberts is now a famous man which he does not think amounts to a whole lot: 'I just want to be getting on with my life's ambition of making the world a better place for horses.' As I said at the beginning: Monty Roberts is an Extra-Ordinary man.

[4]

'Well, Willy, lad, I never thought to see you stuck for words,' said Jack. Of course he is quite right – renowned for my rapier-like wit, master of the snappy riposte – on this occasion I was gobsmacked, flummoxed, banjaxed and reduced to standing there, opening and shutting my mouth like a goldfish.

It had all started quite innocently. Hounds had just caught their fox and there was a lull in the proceedings. I had wandered over to Jack and Ian's Land Rover for a bit of 'crack' and maybe for a sip of something. Ian is a famous composer and musician in the old traditional Northumbrian style. This is the tradition handed down through the generations of pipers and fiddlers in the lonely hill steadings. It is an aural tradition. Even today, a lot of these fine composers and performers neither read nor write music. The music is all in their heads and their fingers – they can 'hold a tune'. Ian's only break with this tradition is that he uses an electronic keyboard on which he is an absolute wizard.

Any road, there was I, leaning in through the window of the Land Rover with a thirsty glint in my eye and Ian says that I should just listen to this. He put a tape in the deck and switched on. There is a vast number of Northumbrian tunes – reels, hornpipes, laments, rants – they tend to be written about places and people and events, as it might be 'Rothbury Hills', 'Whittingham Green Lane', 'The Drops of Brandy', 'The Morpeth Rant', 'Proudlock's Hornpipe'. I can recognise many of the tunes now, even if I cannot always put the right names to them. The tune that was playing I did not recognise, but I thought it a jolly good reel-ly sort of tune.

'I don't recognise that,' said I.

'I've no but just composed it,' said Ian.

'It's a canny tune,' said I. 'What's it called?' Ian and Jack both started laughing.

'Man,' said Jack, 'that's your tune – that's "Willy Poole's Reel",' and that is when I was struck dumb.

Well, I tell you, it is a very canny tune and if Her Gracious Majesty hauled me down to the Palace tomorrow and tapped me on the shoulder with the breadknife, I would not feel as flattered or honoured as I am to have my own reel.

NOTE 'Willy Poole's Reel' may be heard on the 'Talking Book' tape of *The Backwoodsman's Year* and very nice it sounds, too. *See* the Appendix for the publisher's address.

[5]

To supper with Joe and Hannah Hutton. Joe is the doyen of Northumbrian Pipers. For those of you not familiar with the Northumbrian Pipes, they are 'Small Pipes' (bagpipes). The bag is inflated by a little pair of bellows, held by a waist belt and worked by the right elbow. These pipes have a lovely gentle mellow sound and were designed for playing indoors in the long winter evenings before these were polluted by television. Joe has played the pipes since he was a boy. Like so many of the great pipers, Joe was a shepherd. The last eighteen years of his working life were spent at Rowhope, a hard and lonely farm that runs up to the spine of the Cheviots and a place of terrible storms. There was the night that Joe only just made it home, after being out in a blizzard. His coat was stiff as a board with iced snow and his hands frozen. Hannah had to chip the ice off before she could undo the buttons. Ill health eventually forced Joe to retire. The Huttons now live in a snug little house in Rothbury, but their hearts are still out in the hills with the sheep and the hard wild life. The old days are remembered in their tunes and songs.

I had long looked forward to that evening, not just for Joe's piping but because I lusted after some of Hannah's songs. Hannah has a beautiful voice. So we sat after supper, with a dram and the pipe drawing nicely, and listened to some wonderful playing and singing. I even took a turn myself and the Huttons were very polite about it. It was a marvellous evening and I came away with the memory of a real treasure, a song called 'The Key Above The Door': no one sings it like Hannah.

NOTE Since I wrote this piece, Joe Hutton has died. He was a great man, a great piper and quite simply one of the nicest men that I have known. He is greatly missed, but his music lives on and we still have Hannah's wonderful singing to be thankful for.

[6]

We are all very fond of the old General. He makes an excellent Chairman (no one would dare call him a 'Chair') of the Committee. He keeps a rigorous time limit on meetings because he always dines at 20.00 hours sharp. The meetings usually start at 18.30 hours. Should any of the more verbose members be still wittering on at 19.45, they will be brought up sharp by the General saying: 'Thank-you-Jim-any-other-business-good-then-

I-declare-this-meeting-closed' and he will have the minute book under his arm and be out of the door like a greyhound from the trap.

Now the General is a traditionalist. We were all rather surprised, therefore, when, over a pre-meeting dram, he announced that he was buying a caravan. 'Jolly useful,' he said. 'I mean, so few of one's friends have servants these days and they live in such poky little houses, it's a job to go and visit them.' The assembled company mulled this one over in silence. You have to know the General to appreciate just how difficult it was for us to imagine him in a caravan. Indeed, we begged leave to doubt that he had ever set foot in such a thing, except when taking drinks off purveyors of farm machinery at the Muxworthy Agricultural Show.

But what really boggled our collective mind was the thought of him on the road with a caravan in tow. The old man drives like a one-man armoured division. His farm manager once ejected himself from the cab of a tractor which the General was driving, with a laden grain trailer behind, down a steep hill – in top gear. At last, a very bold Gin and Tonic did venture to ask if he intended to tow it himself.

'Certainly not! I shall send a man down with it the day before and then Maudie and I will motor down in the Bentley. Capital idea! You should all do it.'

'But,' said a brave Half of Bitter, 'we haven't all got men to drive the thing for us.'

The General bristled: 'You've all got wives or girlfriends, haven't you? Send them instead.'

[7]

I have an audio cassette that has given me immense pleasure over the last two years. It is called the 'Canniest Place on Eorth' (sic) by Robert Allen. Mr Allen is seventy-three, a retired farmer and a poet whose heroes include Burns, Kipling and Hardy. He likes poems with rhyme and metre and disapproves of this 'moderun slavver' (modern drivel). 'It may be an art form in itself, but it shouldn't pinch the name of poetry.' Mr Allen is undoubtedly a poet and in 1973 he started writing poetry in the North Tyne dialect. He writes about the countryside, farming and events in and around his home town of Bellingham (Bellingjum, please). They are brilliant: funny, sad and very sharp. He has just produced a new tape: 'Ridin' High' on which the eponymous first track must be a comedy classic. I have to warn you that the North Tyne dialect will seem pretty impenetrable at first, with the thick Saxon HR sound (hround the hrugged hrocks), but the more you listen, the more you will tune in and enjoy these clever poems. This cassette will put a real breath of Northumbrian air in your stocking, so: Howway Man! get it browt, I doubt but they'll be sharp selled.

See the Appendix for details from where you may get these tapes.

[8]

Not much common ground (no play on words intended) between myself and Ms Kate Ashbrook – the Head Honcha of the Ramblers' Association. But I heard her on the wireless the other morning and she had a splendid suggestion. She was talking about military training areas and the rights of ramblers to go there and get blown up if they wanted to. She said (and I quote): 'Certainly computer simulation provides a lot of opportunities for training, which does (sic) not require large expanses of open country.' Of course, what the lady had in mind was instead of a lot of squaddies yomping about in the cold and wet, they could all be sitting in the NAAFI with those funny helmets on, zapping tanks from Agoraphobia (or whatever the enemy is called) by 'Virtual Reality'.

Now let us apply a little lateral thinking to this idea on the principle of 'what is sauce for the goose is sauce for the gander'. It does seem to me that 'computer simulation' could just as well be applied to the ramblers, so that they would 'not require large expanses of open country'. Just think about it – they could put on their big boots, their hairy legs and their anoraks, then they could sit in their armchairs with their helmets on – a packet of crisps in one hand (they can drop the packet on the carpet) and a can of brown ale in the other. They can then switch on and ramble wheresoever they wish. We could have the machine programmed so that they could leave gates open and knock down some walls at will. They could even have helmets with a bobble on the top.

This seems to me to be a thoroughly satisfactory way of solving the access problem. Well done, Ms Ashbrook!

[9]

Once upon a time and long, long ago, when both the world and I were quite a bit younger, I went to call on Mr Jan Stewer, a farmer who lived at Stoppadon. He had a renowned strain of Silver Duckwing gamecocks and I wanted a new stud cock. Mr Stewer lived out on the edge of the known world, right up behind Muxworthy, which you have never heard of, thereby proving the point. Not many visitors made it through to Stoppadon. I was made welcome and given a good ham tea by the mountainous, but cheerful, lady of the house. Mr Stewer and I then settled down with mugs of cider on either side of the kitchen range, to set the world to rights and do a little business. Whilst we were talking, Mrs Stewer appeared with an old-fashioned tin hip bath which she put down in front of the fire. Stoppadon drew its water from a well and was lit by oil lamps. Mrs Stewer began to fill the bath with cans of hot water from the boiler built into the old black range.

Mr Stewer paid no attention to these goings-on, nor did his conversation falter when the goodwife started to remove what was obviously the first of many layers of garments. In those days I was very young and very easily embarrassed. I began to feel more than a little superfluous to what was obviously going to be a very domestic scene. The removal of layer no. 2 produced considerable panic in my fledgling breast. I suggested that my departure should be imminent.

Mr Stewer rejected this idea: 'No, no! 'tees all right, Boy, you bide where you'm too: just you move along the seat a bit and 'er'll never splash 'ee from there.'

3. SPRING

[1]

At the time of writing spring is springing. The curlews and the oyster catchers have come in from the coast. Their wild whistling and piping serves the same purpose for me as a canary does for a miner: as long as I can hear it in the spring, then I know the air is safe to breathe. Once 'civilisation' drives out the curlews, then it will be time for me to pack my red spotted handkerchief and move on. Mind you, there are not the curlews about that there used to be. Just over the hill behind my farm there is a large old pasture field that I have always called 'The Curlew Field'. I remember standing in the road one summer morning talking to the wife of the owner and watching whilst a dozen or twenty curlews wheeled and piped above the thick grass. The lady said that the field was famous as a nesting spot. The other morning, I drove up to the field and stopped to watch and listen – nothing – not a sign of a curlew.

It is not just curlews. When we first built the house, lapwings were a common sight and sound through the little valley below us; now we are very nearly a lapwing-free zone. Much has been written about the disappearance of the skylark and I am sorry to say that the same sad state applies here.

Why should this be? I cannot tell you. What I can tell you is that the decline of all these birds has coincided with the sharp rise of the local raptor population – both sparrowhawks and goshawks.

I suppose that it is about five years since that the first goshawks spread into this area from Kielder. How the goshawks (which had been extinct) got to Kielder in the first place is quite another story. I know the story of how it was done, in apparent contravention of the Wildlife and Countryside Act, but if you want to know then I suggest that you direct your enquiries to the RSPB. I understand that they are aware of the circumstances.

I have no proof that the decline of the curlews, lapwings and larks has anything to do with the increase in hawks, but hawks must eat and they are surely not vegetarians.

The grass is greening and we are whizzing about chain harrowing and fertiliser spreading. The auction of my grazing happens in the middle of April and the grass wants to be looking good by then.

Everywhere there are signs of new growth and rebirth. The new plantation behind the old sitka spruce belt is three years old now and is really beginning to look like a young wood. I go along the side of it every morning on my rounds and every morning there is a new burgeoning of delicate new leaf. The ash is going to come in several lengths clear of the oak in the Leaf Stakes this year: 'Ash before oak, we're in for a soak'. A soak would be no bad thing either. We have had no serious rain since the end of January. Some of the thinner soiled hills are starting to turn brown already which does not bode well for later. Water: the use and the waste of it is going to be a problem that will boil over in the '90s [I told you so]. You will all have to give up hosing down the garden gnomes and have water meters fitted.

The dry weather has been wonderful for the heather burning and great clouds of pungent scented smoke have been hanging over the hills. Burning is an essential part of heather husbandry. Old heather becomes tough and stemmy. It is the sweet young shoots that both sheep and grouse like. Someone once asked me why the heather was not cut instead of being burned? Cutting would not be terribly easy on a 1-in-2 hillside strewn with boulders, but if you want to go up there with your secateurs, then be my guest.

Another hectare of woodland has been planted at the top of the quarry and, on the bank below, the gorse and broom are spreading in a most satisfactory manner. In a few more years, there should be enough cover on the farm to hold foxes. I would dearly love to see hounds find a fox in my whins.

There is a self-help feeder by the pond. It has a T-bar on the bottom and if you waggle it with your beak, it drops a stream of wheat. Derek the Muscovy drake is a dab hand at working the system. I have certainly seen the mallard at the feeder, but have not yet seen one working it. There are three pairs on the pond every morning and high hopes of nests on the island. It is time to declare war on the corbies (carrion crows), otherwise they will get the eggs.

The scuttling little moorhens are also back. There are two pairs of partridges in the rough grass by the burn. The marsh has had withies planted all round it and there is no more delicate shade of green than the first sprung willow leaf and, what is more, we have a mass of frog spawn.

Hooray for Spring! It's in the air, in the step and in the blood and I smell bacon for breakfast.

[2]

There is bad news for those who insist that the fox exists entirely on nut cutlets and berry burgers. These gentle people refuse to accept that the fox is a killer for food and, on occasion, for sheer wanton pleasure. The question of foxes and lambs has been responsible for a lot of promiscuous halitosis. The Veggie Brigade have always stoutly maintained that foxes do not eat lambs and even if they do, they only eat dead lambs and, anyway, there would not be any dead lambs if only those cruel, lazy farmers looked after their sheep properly.

The farmer might point out that every lamb lost is a cut in his income and an affront to his stockman's pride but, as the poor beggar is halfway through lambing and half mad from exhaustion, his reply is likely to be more pithy than printable. At last the farmers have had a chance of making a measured response.

The Field magazine sent a questionnaire to 11,000 members of the National Sheep Association. The results were analysed by the Oxford Research Bureau. The findings were (1) that 33% of the farmers who responded had actually seen foxes kill lambs; (2) 54% said that fox control affected livestock predation; (3) 64% of those who replied felt that traditional foxhunting was the most effective method of controlling fox numbers. This percentage rose to 70% in Wales, and the percentage was even higher (72%) in the north.

I have no doubt that there are those who will seek to rubbish this survey, but it only emphasises what country people have always known. The fact that most farmers support hunting is hardly news. Without that grass-roots support for hunting (both as a sport and as a practical method of culling), it would have disappeared long since. Those who bleat at this survey are those who find that it contradicts their cherished prejudices. Prejudices are like underpants; they should be changed regularly.

★

[3]

The first of April brought the start of the roe buck season, but not better weather. It was still black and bitter pre-dawn when I drove up into one of my forested beats, high in the hills. Almost immediately, I saw a nice buck in my headlights. He froze on the ride and I watched him for quite a minute (it is neither legal nor sporting to shoot deer from a vehicle) until he bounded off. I wished him well and hoped he was an omen for the day. He was not, but then again, perhaps he was. For some five hours the dog and I crept about the forest. I saw no less than eleven does, but not another buck was to be seen. In the end, I thought 'b****r it' and sat in the shelter of a rock watching a doe and her female yearling feeding in the basin below me, with the sun now warm on my back and the pipe drawing nicely. Then I went home. Deer – 12; Poole and dog – 0, but then it was April Fool's day.

A question that I cannot answer.

I shot a roe doe the other day, and remember that does are out of season. I had stalked for two hours and seen several does but no bucks. I was walking back to the van and breakfast. My route was down a wide fire-break. There was a strong wind blowing at my back. As I was walking down-wind and the wind was carrying my taint in front of me, I was not attempting to stalk. Just from habit I stopped and glassed the ground in front of me. The little doe was standing just in the edge of the trees about seventy yards away and was looking at me. The dog and I were in full view and she must have got my scent full and clear. I expected her to evaporate into the trees. Instead she moved out into the centre of the fire-break and stood side on – a perfect presentation for a shot – staring straight at me. I was then able to get a proper look at her. I use good Zeiss binoculars and I could see every detail. She still had her ragged winter coat and I could see that she was a walking skeleton. Still she stood. I had a hard decision to make – suppose she had a kid. I opened my bipod stick and said out loud,

'If you haven't moved by the time I have you in the sights, I will shoot you.' She never moved. I took the shot and she dropped where she stood.

She was yeld (barren) – that was a relief. She was just a rickle of bones covered in skin. Her liver was riddled with fluke and terribly abscessed. She must have been suffering horribly. She was dying by the 'natural means' that some conservationists advocate – Nature culls by disease and starvation.

I had heard stalkers' tales of suffering deer presenting themselves to be shot, but stalkers can be a bit like fishermen and *cum grano salis* is a handy phrase. Did that little doe present herself for a quietus? She had every chance to make herself scarce. Did she seek me out, or was it coincidence? I do not know. All I know is that I gave her a quick, clean end to her suffering and I am proud of that.

[4]

Whenever I struggle off train or plane, red eyed, haggard, shaking and probably snuffling from some ghastly lergy picked up in the south, the first thing that I do is to take the dogs and do a tour of the farm, to see what has changed. At this time of year, there are daily changes. There is the first delicate touch of green on the hawthorn. The clamour from the rookery behind the house is increasing. The pair of partridges are back in the rough grass of the new plantation – they reared a brood of thirteen last year. There is a young Scots pine with tatters of bark hanging from a fresh white scar – the little roe buck has been fraying with his horns.

Down in the shallows by the bulrushes there is a noise like a small machine shop. If you approach very quietly a mass of little dark heads will stop what they are doing and look up warily – the frogs are at it like journalists. We planted some more withies in the marsh this year and the first greeny white buds are showing. Within the next month they should be a mass of tender green leaves.

The gorse in the quarry is blooming determinedly – not that it is ever without a few flowers – 'when gorse is out of bloom, kissing's out of season' and we certainly cannot have that. In a few weeks, the whins will be a mass of old gold.

The hares are boxing; there are fox cubs in the badger sett; the golden plover and curlews are in on the hill. Spring is springing, but watch out, the snow is still lingering in the deep sykes 'out-bye'; more could come at any time.

[5]

The fields are full of ewes and young lambs. At this early stage, what I believe we must now call the 'bonding process' between ewe and lamb may still be in a fragile state. Some ewes are more maternal than others. An occasional ewe is so unmaternal that its offspring have to be 'taken into care' and fostered. Misfit ovine (sic) mums do not get extensive counselling at the taxpayers' expense; they become curry vindaloo. There is an interesting thought for the 'over-stretched social services'.

Ewes with single lambs are little problem. Most ewes have twins and some have threes and it is important that the bonding process is reinforced at regular intervals. It is the shepherd's (me) job to see that all is well, morning and night.

Should you look closely at a field of ewes and lambs you will see that the lambs have strange hieroglyphics painted on them, as it might be G3 or ****. Each pair of lambs is marked the same. In the course of things, lambs, when playing or asleep in the sun, get separated from their mothers. Thus, the shepherd on his round may find little G1 (the bane of my life at the moment) 'alone and palely loitering'. He catches the waif with his lambing stick and looks about him. There is a pair of $$ grazing happily with their mother. There is a single %7 tucking into the teat and, yes, the little chap just prodded to his feet is the other %7 and he is soon in for his tucker as well. Nowhere is there a sign of another G1.

So the shepherd puts G1 under his arm, or in his bag, and wanders on his round. Every now and then he gives a shrill whistle through his teeth. This is the 'Mother-up' signal. The ewes run blaring, looking for their sleeping/playing offspring and telling them to come home for their tea this instant or the bogeyman will get them. Lambs will come running to the sound and dash in under the ragged fleece, bumping the udder to get the milk down. The ewe gives each one a careful sniff; no gatecrashers allowed. Recognition is all by smell and sound.

G1 gives a bleat and a wriggle. He is hungry and lonely and wants his mummy. Way down the hedgeback is a wild-looking ewe with a single lamb. As soon as she sees the shepherd approaching, she is looking for off, with the lamb scampering behind her, but the dog bars her path, grinning as he fixes her with his 'eye'. The lamb on the ground is marked G1. The shepherd puts his G1 lamb down and it totters off to its mother. She sniffs it briefly as it dives underneath, but she is very busy stamping at the dog. The shepherd waits until the lamb is sucking well, its tail wagging with pleasure. This is all part of the 'mothering up' process: it somehow sounds cosier than bonding.

'Low input sustainable agricultural practices' is a fine sounding phrase, but what does it actually mean? I will lay an example on you. A few years ago I was in New Zealand where all farm subsidies have been abolished and low input farming has to be. I was discussing lambing practices with a farmer and telling him how my lambing ewes were checked continuously throughout the twenty-four hours and given every assistance should a natal delivery be difficult. Now it should be remembered that this man was running some 8,000 ewes with one shepherd (low inputs, you understand). They rode their 'lambing beat' which took several hours once a day. What about assisting a difficult lambing? I asked. He replied that if they had to help a bloody ewe, then they chopped an ear off the bloody ewe at the same time and that was her marked for the bloody cannery. Now is that low input and sustainable enough for you?

[6]

One of the many nice spin offs from the planting we have done on the farm, the increasing cover in the fledgling garden and the number of nest boxes put up has been a tremendous increase in birds of all sorts, from the blackbird who imitates my wife whistling for the dogs, through the three thrushes nesting in the garden, past numerous tits of all denominations, via robins and finches various down to the utterly splendid little goldcrests. We encourage them with feeders and watch their backs as best we can by declaring war on the corby crows and keeping no cats.

I have never had much time for cats. Incontinent cat is one of the nastiest and most lingering smells that I know. I was a farm student once at a house from which my boss had recently evicted his mother, his two sisters and as many of their cats as he could cram into the car. He then spent a week sitting outside the french windows with a bottle of gin ('new every morning') and a .22 rifle. Forty-eight cats were 'terminated with extreme prejudice', but their memory lingered on in the house.

It is estimated (who on earth does all these estimations?) that domestic pussies kill some 20 million small birds every year. So those of you who continually bemoan the decline of our songbird population now have a simple answer: you need a bottle of gin, a .22 rifle and . . .

[7]

The swallows were flying low this morning when I went round the stock. I stopped to watch and marvel. Swallows are some of the most amazing performers on the wing: the banks, the long slow glides, the ability to stall suddenly in mid flight and hang almost motionless for a split second as they seize some unseen insect; the swift swoops under full power; the ability to do 180-degree turns, at speed and seemingly in their own lengths. It was truly a sight to enjoy and wonder at and it made me late for breakfast, which is no big deal these days, just a cup of tea waved under the nose, me having been told to lose a stone in weight and all.

It is always a pleasure to watch birds in flight. We now have a rookery in the shelter belt behind the house. This is a new development (I like to think of it as Executive Housing) and we feel rather honoured, in spite of the noise at corvine bedtime. We all remember the clichéd phrase about 'rooks cawing in the immemorial elms'. There are not any elms around here and the shelter belt is sitka spruce and this led to certain initial design flaws in the nest building. The rooks built their first nests high on the west-facing side of the wood. Sitka are bendy trees, so when the first decent westerly gale came whooping in, the tree tops whipped about and the newly constructed nests went east. The rooks built again, high on the east side. A nasty gale came in off the North Sea and this time the nests went west. 'It's dogged as does it': the rooks then built lower down and in the comparatively sheltered middle of the wood where they are no doubt being fruitful and multiplying.

Having our own rooks, as it were, means that I can look out of my office window and watch them riding the thermals in the little valley below the house, spiralling upwards like a cloud of black smuts in the updraught of a bonfire. They are a blasted nuisance because they waste my time when I should be writing about them instead of watching them. I have had to blank off part of the window, but I can still see the nut feeder outside the kitchen window. At the moment there are three greenfinches fighting a spectacular aerial battle over access to the nuts, whilst a bluetit and a great tit have taken advantage of the situation to pop in for a bite.

When my office window is open, a wren often comes to visit. It pops in under the window and perches on the sill, turning its head from side to side as it studies the strange fat man tapping away at his machine only an arm's length away. Wrens are my favourite small birds and there was a brood of them reared in the garden.

Amongst the nesting boxes we have scattered around the farm are two palatial owl boxes which remain sadly empty. Something like one-sixth of the farm has gone down to trees (mixed woodland). I suppose that that, the pond and the wild area surrounding it has meant a more favourable 'habitat'; a word that always makes me think of the sort of chairs that I do not fit in. It is unfortunate that the avian increase includes an increase in corbies on whom war must now be declared. They have cleaned out at least one duck's nest down by the pond and I am not having that.

And, finally

I stayed at Cliveden not very long ago. It is now a hotel and a very, very good one. The house once belonged to the Dukes of Sutherland. Carefully preserved in a glass case is a Y-shaped stick. This is 'Harriet, Duchess of Sutherland's Pushing-Up-Hill Stick'. It is a steep pull from the river to the house. The dowager was a big lady. So a footman of the brawnier sort was detailed to come behind her and, by applying the stick in the right place, provide a little uphill propulsion.

4. NOT JUST A JOB BUT A WAY OF LIFE

[1]

Fancy a job with plenty of travel, seventeen weeks' holiday a year, comfortable accommodation, plus three square meals per day all found and working as part of a close-knit team? That made you prick your ears up.

Fancy a job where you are away from home and its comforts for ten weeks at a time, where you work irregular hours, where you are subject to some of the worst weather conditions available, where the work can be dangerous, not least because you spend your working hours on a floating bomb? Not quite so keen now, perhaps?

What we are talking here is the coastal tanker trade and if you do not know much about it, then neither did I, but I went to find out.

The launch was bucking and pitching in the Atlantic swell that was rolling into Milford Haven. The long grey sea-worn shape of the anchored ship was emerging from the wrack and the spray. The launch man picked up the RT hand set: '*Alacrity, Alacrity* – which side do you want me on?' The set crackled: 'The swell's just as nasty either side,' said a cheerful voice. 'Oh sh*t!' I said. As I climbed out onto the frantic foredeck of the launch and looked up at the sheer side of the ship and the rope ladder that was being unrolled down it, I said it again – with feeling.

F. T. Everard & Sons Ltd are one of the few British shipping firms left. A family firm since 1922, it operates a fleet of coastal tankers and dry cargo ships carrying things like road stone, malting barley and china clay. The 'Itty Boats' – as they were known locally – coming in to load china clay at Fowey were part of my childhood. The names of the ships of the Everard Line nearly all end in -ity – *Sagacity, Capacity, Assiduity* (known to the Cornish as Acidity). Legend has it that the names were chosen by Miss Ethel Everard (daughter of the owner and founder) from *Nuttalls Standard Pronouncing* [Sic] *Dictionary*.

The M.V. *Alacrity* is a 3,345-tonne multi-purpose tanker, four years old and built to a Norwegian design that Everards purchased. Her main deck is a bewildering (to me) array of pipes, valves and manifolds. The two-storeyed engine room is aft and below decks. Above this rises the three-storeyed superstructure which houses the cabins, the galley and the messroom. On top is the bridge. She has a crew of seven – Master, two mates, two engineers, cook/ able seaman, deck hand and a trainee. The strong hands that snatched me from the waves belonged to Sean Bell (Deck Hand) and Chris Hyde (Trainee).

Paul Darton (Master – 'The Old Man') is a lovely man with a

grey beard and a twinkling eye. He is a lifelong mariner. He runs his ship with a sure but light touch. The *Alacrity* (cheerful readiness – *Chambers Dictionary*) is a happy ship – ('We're always ready and sometimes cheerful'). With him on the bridge was John Pratt, the Chief Engineer, a large quiet man with a dry humour.

A modern bridge is an eye opener to anyone expecting teak wheels and big brass engine-room telegraphs. It is a mass of radar screens, glowing lights and push buttons – everything can be controlled by one man with one finger, but you have still got to know how to get where you are going.

Alacrity was anchored in the bay waiting for a berth to load for Poole in Dorset. The cargo would be 1,030 tons unleaded petrol, 570 tons 4-star petrol, 600 tons of road diesel and 330 tons of gas oil when she got the berth. She had already been waiting for twenty-four hours. I was introduced to that other essential bit of bridge equipment, the electric kettle, and made myself the first of a long line of cups of tea.

The bridge was also the social centre of the ship: the crew drifted in and out in a cloud of banter. Next to appear was Jane Ward, the Second Engineer. A woman? I hear you cry and why not, pray? Jane has been at sea for four years.

But it was 1700, time for dinner and to meet that most important man – the Cook. It is impossible to overestimate the importance of the Cook to the morale of the ship. The crew reminisced about 'Bacteria Bill', 'The Penzance Poisoner' and the Lithuanian who used to paint his feet instead of wearing socks. Taff Harries, from Haverfordwest, is a genius. In his tiny galley he commits wonderful acts of culinary delight. His treacle pudding is the stuff of wicked dreams. The fridge is open to all comers to make themselves a snack whenever they feel like it.

At dinner I met Mamun Rahman – Second Officer and from Bangladesh. He was wistful about curry but was stowing the treacle pud away, no bother.

Jane's cigarette set the fire alarm off.

And so to bed: twenty years ago I sailed on a ship on which the crew accommodation approximated to a BR second class sleeper:

things are very different now. Even a crewman has a comfortable single cabin with its own shower, wash basin and 'heads'.

Day 2:

0700 and still at anchor. On the previous night Paul had hoped to be at the berth by 0715. It was not to be. 'About 1300,' said the shore. There was nothing for it but one of Taff's 'Cholesterol Specials' – eggs, bacon, sausages, beans, mushrooms, toast . . . oh dear! oh dear!

We watched our sister ship, the *Agility*, heading out of the estuary for Belfast. Our loading time was put back to 1600, but there was Taff's Chilli con Carne for luncheon. It seems that there can be a lot of waiting in the shipping business. Sean once sat on ship off Algiers for four and a half months. It is small wonder that sailors develop hobbies (apart from the now ubiquitous television and videos). Jane does tapestry and the Master makes model boats.

All the time, other ships in the haven were weighing anchor and heading in for their berths. Our loading time had now gone back to 2200. Ah well, there was 'Snake and Pygmy' pie, spuds, cauliflower, carrots, fruit crumble and ice cream for dinner.

2215 and up anchor at last and up the darkening river to where the refineries were lit up like huge Christmas trees. But the other ship was still on the berth. She had been there for two and a half days for a normal loading time of twelve hours. Truth will out. Our predecessor had been carrying tallow and had failed to wash out her tanks properly, so that when she had been loaded with petrol and the cargo was tested for 'spec' it was found to be contaminated. The whole lot had to be pumped out, cleaned and reloaded – a very expensive process: 'Someone's going to get their arse in a sling.'

2325 and we were alongside the berth, with its loading derricks crouched above us like escapees from Jurassic Park. The pipes were connected and the pumping began.

Day 3:

0530 and we were loaded. 'Everything goes well when it's warm and dry,' said Terry McDowell, the Chief Officer. He had joined us at the berth having been ashore getting treatment for a bad back. He has been with Everards for eleven years: 'Or since 1834,' said Paul.

0645 we cast off from the berth. The *Alacrity* has 300-hp bowthrusters and an 'Ulstein High Lift Rudder'. All of this means that she is highly manoeuvrable and, in skilled hands, can go sideways and turn almost in her own length. As Paul is 'ticketed' for Milford Haven, because he uses it so often, the *Alacrity* can come and go without a Pilot.

0705 and we were past the Esso buoy and heading into a thick drizzly sea mist. As we passed the anchored, waiting ships, the crew made scathing comments about them: 'We don't think we're the best; we know we're the best.' As we passed St Anne's Head, the fog horn was booming. Cholesterol time: 'More mushrooms ordered'; 'Not mushroom for anything else.' As far as I was concerned that situation was soon to change.

The passage to Poole is simple on paper: 97.5 miles to Land's End (heading 199), come onto 180 for 12½ miles to enter traffic separation lanes; 31½ miles to the Lizard on 095; 64 miles to Start Point on 076; 71 miles to the Anvil on 068, then 010 across Lyme Bay for 5 miles; it should take about twenty-eight hours. But there is an awful lot of water under those statistics. A great deal of that water was coming in from the Atlantic in a huge rolling swell. *Alacrity* butted and corkscrewed her way through, with great curls of green water crashing over her foc's'le ('Mind you, this stretch can be a bit naughty in winter'). The *Alacrity* rides low in the water with a load on and the main deck is always a-wash.

The mates and the deck crew who had been up most of the night with the loading turned in. There is no hard and fast watch system with a small crew, but the normal procedure on a passage is that the Captain has the bridge during the day and the Mates split the night between them. Paul is a most entertaining companion with tales about other days and old times at sea, when the

'Old Man' was like God, there was no air conditioning and the cockroaches used to nibble the dead skin off your feet whilst you slept. It all helped keep my mind off my inner disquietude. The cellphone rang: the caller wanted Jim because he was stuck on the M25 and would be late; where were we? 'In the Atlantic'; 'Bloody Nora!' said the man and rang off.

The coastguard came on the RT to say that there was a Mayday call. It was well to the north, somewhere in the Irish Sea. 'Probably a yacht': the Captain has strong feelings about yachties, ferry captains ('Timetables instead of brains') and fishermen, all of whom have come close to causing him grief in his time. If you are driving a tanker, the consequences of a collision could cause a very great deal of grief. At this point I was overcome by a little private grief and took to my bunk. Even the thought of Taff's tuna fish cakes and fruit pie failed to console me and . . .

17.30 we were off Land's End, the sun was shining, I was mightily purged and we passed the Wuff-wuff (The Wolf Rock to you). The excesses of the Atlantic were exchanged for the calmer waters of the Channel. The change in the mood of the crew was noticeable. We were overtaken by a large, homeward-bound Russian cargo ship. Her hatch covered a parking place for assorted cars and vans – a little capitalist enterprise on the part of the crew. As we crossed Mounts Bay, a pair of yachties gossiping on the RT got a right rollocking from Falmouth Coastguard for taking up an emergency channel – really! yachties! We passed the Lizard Point lighthouse in the dimpsey. 'It's evenings like this that make it all worthwhile,' said John as we leant on the wing of the bridge. I managed an apple and turned in. The rest of the crew had gone to ground to watch *Red Dwarf*.

Day 4:
0630: we were sailing along the path of the rising sun on an oily calm between Start Point and Portland Bill. Cherbourg Coastguard was getting ratty with somebody who would not talk to it. It seems that someone had been making farmyard noises at

Cherbourg and it was cross: 'I expect it's the Filipinos.' 'Do they do a lot of that?' 'They always get the blame.'

The Flintstones accompanied breakfast in the Mess Room: 'They put them on specially for kids and merchant seamen.' Anvil Point and Durlestone Point slipped by to port and Bournemouth appeared in the distance. There were yachts everywhere and the radar screen was spattered: 'Keep your eyes open for all those damn boats.'

Jane was welding in the engine room and set the fire alarm off.

A large 'Gin Palace' appeared to be intent on playing 'chicken' with *Alacrity*, but sheered off at the last moment. We could see that the lady helm-person was receiving some very intimate instruction – what you might call 'hands on experience'.

Now, another problem: our berth in Poole was occupied by the *Ghent*, which had nipped in to load a cargo of styrene. We would have to anchor. 'It's four years since we've had to do this.' 'It's having a journalist on board.' 'A Jonah, that's what he is.' Paul said that if they did not behave he would sing the Tigger Song (from *Winnie the Pooh*). This threat produced instant discipline. Never mind, we had the Poole Yacht Club Regatta to watch.

1320: the Pilot came aboard. The deep-water channel into Poole harbour is narrow and tortuous and full of yachts of all shapes, sizes, and degrees of proficiency. *Alacrity* edged her way through and eventually the dock came in sight. The *Ghent*, now loaded, was budging up on the wharf to make room for us, astern of a Dutch ship manned by the 'Holy Willies' – a strict sect who will not work on Sundays and have to anchor from Saturday night until Monday morning.

1400 and all secure on the berth and unloading ready to commence. Then it would be back to Milford Haven – Poole – Milford Haven – Falmouth . . . day in, day out, ten weeks on and five off. I do not envy the crew of the *Alacrity*, but for them it is not just a job but a way of life and they do it with, well, alacrity.

★

[2]

It turned out to be an interesting morning. I had been slightly miffed when I arrived at the wood gate at 0430 to find the track blocked by an assortment of vans and caravans. My first thought was that some travellers had somehow strayed into this remote spot, but then I saw the helicopter and reasoned that they would be very 'New Age' indeed to boast an air cavalry section. There was no one about to ask, so I went up the other track instead, resolving to sort the mystery out later.

Anyway, it was about 0800 when I got back to the van and my breakfast. Whilst I was eating I could see the encampment coming to life, so I lit the pipe and went round to introduce myself. It turned out that the travellers were a team from Dollar Helicopters who were there to do some aerial fertilising for the Forestry Commission. I thought that this was bound to be worth watching so I drove high up on the side of Hedgehope (2,300 feet) where I could look down on the area in question.

In the forest I met Jonathan Farries from Forest Enterprises who explained what was happening. Analysis of foliage samples from this particular block of trees had shown a deficiency in phosphate and potash so this was to be applied in granular form at a rate of 650 kgs per hectare. A stack of 750-kg bags of 'Scotphos' had been made in a clearing. The team had a series of hopper/spreaders each of which held 750 kgs, so each hopper load would cover just over a hectare. The hoppers were loaded by a small crane worked by the two-man ground crew. The helicopter came in and hovered over the hopper with a dangling hook. This was snecked onto the hopper and hooray-and-up-she-rises. When the pilot was in position, he flipped a switch in the cockpit which operated the spreader motor on the bottom of the hopper. Each load took 2½ minutes to spread.

I suspect that you are wondering just how the pilot knew where to start each run. After all, one block of sitka spruce looks much like another. In the early days of aerial fertilising it was all done visually, by Guess and God, as it were. But now, my children, we have GPS (Global Plotting System), a satellite navigation system that can pinpoint positions to within a few feet. The details of the drop area are fed into a computer and the system tells the pilot exactly when and where to push the button. I imagine that God must always be a factor in low-level flying, but the Guess has now been totally removed from the equation. In this way 27 tonnes were spread with total accuracy and in a very short time.

From my vantage point I watched the helicopter buzzing about below me, like a large, red dragonfly. When the button was pushed the hopper trailed a white cloud that gradually settled into the trees below. Then the chopper would whizz back to the clearing, hover, the empty hopper would be unhooked, a full one put on and away it would go. It was a neat, slick operation. The team (1 pilot, 2 loaders, 1 mechanic, 1 computer operator/logistic expert/cook) travels all over the country on this work. They were going on to Dumfriesshire that day, then on to Southern Ireland for two weeks.

As I said, it was a most interesting and unexpected morning.

[3]

Tony Dove took a bit of finding. We knew that he was somewhere in Kielder Forest, but 60,000 hectares is a lot of somewhere. Even Dr Bob McIntosh, the Forest District Manager, was reluctant to stick a pin in his map and say positively that Tony was there. We had to search. Our quest took us deep into the forest and high up onto the desolate border land between England and Scotland, to the aptly-named Deadwater where the climate is 'nine months of winter and three months' bad weather'. At long last we sighted a Land-Rover and horse trailer parked on a stretch of long-dead railway line. We had located Tony Dove and his horse Clyde. We now knew where they were, but the question was why?

Kielder is the largest man-made forest in Europe and one of

the most efficient. Manual labour is almost a thing of the past. Huge computer-controlled harvesters cut, trim and log trees in one action, doing the daily work of twelve men with chain saws. Great articulated Volvo 'Forwarders' lead the timber out to the hard roads. So where do a man and a horse fit in?

There are Environmentally Sensitive Areas and also areas kept for their amenity value scattered all over the forest. Huge, hi-tech machines would make too much mess extracting timber from these areas. There are also hillsides too steep for even the most rugged machinery. This is where Tony, with Clyde and Prince, his two Clydesdales, come into their own.

Of course, a man would have to be born to this sort of highly skilled work. Tony with his weather-beaten face and loose-kneed hillman's walk looks every inch the countryman born and bred. In fact, he only took over the horse work five years ago when the previous horseman retired. Before that he lived at Burgess Hill and worked in the British Rail Research Department in Muswell Hill in London. He had never been to the North in his life. At the age of fifty, Tony decided to take early retirement. He wanted a rural life and wrote to Dr McIntosh on a whim. He sold his Sussex home at the peak of the market and this enabled him to buy a house in the lonely village of Kielder and set himself up with two horses and the Land-Rover and trailer. He has never been to London since and has never looked back.

Tony had never worked with horses before he came to Kielder. In the early days, he was greatly helped by the retired horseman, David Hudson, who was a well-known Kielder character.

Up at Deadwater, a stand of immature sitka had been felled on what was deemed to be an Environmentally Sensitive Area. The felled trees looked like a huge heap of giant spillikins. 'Looks as though they've had the students working on this one,' said Dr Bob, with a managerial furrow in his brow.

We met Clyde, the nine-year-old, 17-hand Clydesdale; a truly gentle giant. Clyde works with a collar and trace chains. Tony backed him up to the tangle of trees and brash ('No, not there, you silly old bugger, come over') and dropped the rope reins.

Clyde stood quietly. Tony hooked the trace chains onto the triangular-shaped swingle tree, on the apex of which he hooked another chain and took the end with him as he leaped in agile manner amongst the tumbled mass of timber and evil-smelling bog mould. Each load of trimmed tree trunks had to be assembled by hand. The size of each load was judged by eye and never allowed to go to the maximum that Clyde could cope with.

The horse was keen to be off. Tony picked up the reins and clicked his tongue. Clyde set off at a run, his chained load frisking behind him as he squandered through the bog and shot up the steep side of the old railway embankment, then along the track to the growing pile of timber. Thus the work goes for six working hours a day; every day; come rain, hail, sleet or wind (there was plenty of all that day). As Tony said: 'People see us at work in the summer and think what a marvellous job, but you do not see many of them up here in weather like this.'

Tony loves his work and his horses. His day starts at 0645 with feeding and grooming. At 0800 he boxes up the horse – they work alternate days – and is at work by 0830. There is a midday stop for man and horse to eat their bait. Work finishes at about 1530, then it is back to the stable for feed and grooming. He is paid by the ton and reckons the business just about wipes its face, but it is not just a job, it is a way of life.

We were thankful to get back into the shelter of the car. Clyde was standing patiently as Tony hooked up another load: a happy man and a happy horse, in tune with each other and with their work. Then they both disappeared in a horizontal blizzard of sleet.

[4]

1100 at SHS Services Wharf in Rotherham, on the banks of the murky River Don; a string of blunt-ended, ungainly barges tied to the wharf, whilst Cawood Hargreaves tug *No. 107* was fussing another barge (or, as they are known in the business, 'pans') under the loading shoot. A continuous stream of heavy tipping lorries from a nearby open-cast mine were reversing up the ramp and tipping their dusty loads into the pan. Business as usual on South Yorkshire's working waterways (run by British Waterways).

The two Skippers (and the crew) on *107* were Brian Denby and Bill Gillyean. They have worked together for seventeen years and have been on the canals all their lives. Both come from generations of canal people.

A barge train consists of three pans propelled by a 180-horse-power Volvo-engined tug, a no-frills workhorse that looks hideous but can move like a ballet dancer thanks to the fact that its propeller can move through 360 degrees. The total length of the train is 198 feet. Each pan carries c.180 tons of coal. The train, therefore, carries the equivalent of *twenty-five* lorry loads, with minimal fuss, pollution or damage to the environment. The pans and the tug are lashed together to form one rigid unit. The pans are pushed when loaded and pulled when empty. The unloaded pans stand some six feet out of the water and you cannot see through them.

At 1130, the three loaded pans and the tug had been chained and hawsered together and it was time to set out on England's waterways.

It is thirty-six miles of a big loop on rivers and canals from Rotherham to Ferrybridge Power Station. The journey takes thirteen hours laden and is split over two days. The return trip with empty pans takes about five hours. Bill and Brian do three trips a week. They start each morning between 0530 and 0600 and are seldom home before 7 o'clock in the evening. They love their work.

We set off down the Don with Brian at the helm. The helm is just a little finger-tip joy-stick that moves the propeller. That, the gears and the throttle are all the controls required. Bill was up on the pans giving the couplings an extra blessing. He then took a bucket and rope and washed down the walkways on the side of the pans. A sharp turn through a narrow bridge brought us to Aldwarke Lock, the first of seven for the day. The British Water-

ways locks are highly technically efficient and are kept with care
and pride. Tugs and locks are all connected by radio and a good
deal of humorous banter.

The backview of industrial South Yorkshire, as seen from the
canals, was nothing to write to mother about. The canals have a
guaranteed depth of 8 feet 2 inches, but the heavily-laden train
was often scouring the bottom, the propeller churning up some
pretty nasty gunge: 'We're ironing it out as we go along.' This silt
blocks the sea cocks which makes the engine start to heat. Cleaning
the filters is a regular job. Just the thing to give a chap an appetite
for the beefburgers and chips which were handed over at the next
lock. This was washed down with strong cups of tea. Apart from
the tiny wheel-house, the only other cover for the crew was the
little cuddy down below. Here there were seats and an ancient
coal-fired range that roared away all day, with the kettle on the
hob: a bit of welcome warmth from the mean north-east wind
that quickly seeped into the bones of anyone standing on deck.
Thank goodness it was not raining.

You see a different world from the canal and mostly the back
of it; backs of old pubs, old houses, factories new and derelict,
well-kept gardens, scrap yards ('That's scrap: most of it goes in
t' canal and we pick it up in t' prop'). The prop is also fouled by
rubbish – old sacks, plastic sheeting, rope and other things that
you really do not want to hear about . . . The only way to cope
with this is to stop the engine, get the boat hook out and try to
hook the rubbish up. This happened several times during the trip.
The Double Bridges at Mexborough provided a challenge to the
helmsman's skill. Not only were they very narrow, but the train
had to do a shunt to get round a very sharp bend.

After Mexborough the scenery opened up into scattered
countryside where farms mingled with breakers' yard and neat
gardens were interspersed with derelict fields full of ponies. Conisbrough Castle appeared on the skyline and the Don plunged into
a beautiful wooded gorge crossed by the amazing soaring piles of
the Conisbrough Viaduct. Industrial S. Yorkshire might have been
a hundred miles away. Sprotbrough Lock is a local beauty spot

and a favourite for 'Gongoozlers'. This is a canal word for those who like to come and watch water and boats.

As we crossed under the viaduct of the A1, the dusk was falling fast. We passed the grim bulk of the new Doncaster Prison, the river now lit by the lights of the prison and the rail yards, and here we passed from the Don to the Doncaster Canal. At 5 pm we tied up at Long Sandall Lock, our overnight stop. 'Behave yourself tonight, mind,' said Brian who was going home to do some decorating. Brian and Bill both live at Thorne which has a large canal community.

Day 2, 0600: pitch dark and cold when we met again at the lock. Brian was disappointed at my lack of nocturnal exploits. Bill went off to light the stove in the cuddy and barge *No. 107* glided out of the lock and into the darkness.

The daylight came seeping over the flat countryside. Fishermen were already setting up on the banks. Lights reflected in the black mirror of the canal. It was cold. As the light increased, a flock of gulls appeared behind us. The little fish churned up by the prop provide them with breakfast. We crept under the Grimsby–Cleethorpes railway bridge with a couple of inches to spare ('She'll just nicely do it, Brian,' said Bill). There are bridges where the top of the wheelhouse has to be taken down in order to squeeze underneath.

Brian was already on the RT, warning the lift bridge at Barnby Dun of our approach. He was winding up Ian, the bridge keeper, about Rugby League: 'What X? He's rubbish; couldn't tackle a Sunday dinner.' The RT made spluttering noises.

With the full light came Bramwith Junction: turn right for the Trent: turn left, as we did, onto New Junction Canal which runs straight as a pencil to join the Aire and Calder (east for Goole and west for Leeds). The New Junction runs through deeply rural country of flat old pasture fields with thick thorn hedges. A roe buck watched us pass. A mink swam across in front of us. Silent herons lined the banks. There were mallard on the canal with some feral white Aylesbury ducks. At 0730 the smell of frying bacon (is there a better smell on a cold morning?) came whiffling up from the cuddy: Bill had breakfast on the go.

In this flat country, swing bridges are the thing. Jimmy Peters runs from one to another in his van opening them for the tugs. We edged our way over the aqueduct that took us over the River Don. There was confusion on the RT about a supposed train coming the other way. It was eventually agreed as a figment of someone's imagination: 'Happen he had too many pints last neet.' But, at Syke House Lock, *107* pulled in to wait for an oncoming oil tanker heading for Thorpe Marsh Power Station. Apart from the locks and the bridges, there was little sign of human activity in this stretch, except for when we were overtaken by a man giving his horse a pipe opener along the canal bank.

We passed the aqueduct over the River Went and came to the T-junction with the Aire and Calder opposite Northfield reservoir. A row of cormorants sat on a line of navigation markers. On deck, the bitter, sneaky wind seemed to shrivel body and mind. Another cup of tea and a 'feet up' in front of the stove was very welcome.

Our progress was being hampered a bit by activity in the locks at Goole that had drained a great deal of water from the system and brought the level of the canal down by eight inches. It may not sound much, but it made the difference between bumping on the bottom or not.

1015 and Pollington Lock: this time we were going uphill. The pathetic bloated remains of a puppy floated in the lock: they see worse than that on the canals. There was more traffic on this waterway. There was a house/narrow boat following behind us and scattered cabin cruisers heading east.

Up in the bows of the forward pan it was a different world away from the throb of the diesel. The only sound was the bow wave. Bill came and joined me: 'Grand up here, isn't it.' It was, but also very cold. I was glad to get back into the warmth of the wheel house.

The rural nature of the bank side was fading. Kellingley Colliery ('The Big K') came in sight to starboard with the vast towers of Ferrybridge looming in the murk beyond. It was a dreary day and a cup of tea and some hot buttered toast cheered things up.

We were getting near to our destination, but we stopped in the

Knottingley Cut. *Tug 107* was to be serviced, so Brian Gregson and Neil Guest were coming out with an empty train. Brian and Bill would take that back to Rotherham. T'other Brian and Neil would take our train in to the power station. They brought our lunch: ham sandwiches: 'Nice ham but, sorry, no mustard. I licked it all off'. An 'Effluent Disposal Barge' went by; a great aid to appetite.

The sheer size of Ferrybridge Power Station was awesome. Two million tons of coal are brought in by water every year. The loaded pans were dropped off at the power station wharf where they were taken over by a shunting tug. This tug fussed them into a narrow canal where a huge machine like a mechanical elephant took over. It straddled the canal and, with a trumpeting of heavy diesel motors, it dropped its hydraulic trunk and pushed each barge into an underwater platform. This picked up the whole pan, some 200 tons, gripped it, whisked it 100 feet up the face of the dock and upended it, as though it were a coal bucket, into the hoppers behind. This was a truly awesome sight. It took about 15 minutes to empty our pans. They were immediately pushed out of the canal and picked up for the return journey.

I was leaving Brian and Bill to make the return journey to Rotherham while I went home by car. After the peace of the canals, the thunder and stink of the motorway and the blinding spray thrown up by huge lorries made one heartily wish that more of their loads could be transported with minimal fuss and pollution on British waterways. It seems an admirable way of getting the job done. For men like Brian and Bill the barges are not just a job, but a way of life. As Brian said: 'You've never lived if you haven't been on t'canal.'

[5]

Haaf is a Scandinavian word for 'heave'. Haaf netting came to this country with the Vikings and is still used to catch salmon and sea trout in certain places. It happens thus: the haaf net consists of a 15-foot horizontal bar from which a purse net is suspended. At each end of the horizontal bar there is a vertical bar (4ft 4ins) to spread the mouth of the net. In the middle of the horizontal there is another vertical bar that extends above the horizontal, thereby supplying a hand hold for the operator. Any questions so far? Jolly good; carry on.

Forward the operator: here he comes waddling down the beach, with his net over his shoulder. He is waddling because he is wearing chest-high waders, a cocoon of sweaters, a tattered waterproof coat, a battered hat. It is important to have a hat that hides the face from photographers; it all has something to do with HM Inspector of Taxes (Dumfries) who is reported to take a keen interest in haaf netting. With all that clothing it is hard not to waddle and he is dressed like that because, where he is going, it is likely to be cold and wet. Over his shoulder there is a large bag for holding the fish after it has been seen to with the large 'priest' that he carries in his belt.

The operator then wades out and faces into the tide whichever way the tide is running. He unships his net and stands the frame upright in the water so that the net billows out with the tide behind him and around him. He then stands with the murky waters swirling up to his chest, one hand on the centre upright and one testing the net. He then hopes that a salmon will swim into the net. As soon as he feels a fish, the whole net is heaved upwards, rather like a huge shrimping net and Bob's your uncle. Now you see why it is called a haaf (heave) net.

This rather esoteric form of fishing is confined to the Severn Estuary and the Solway Firth or, more particularly, the rivers that run to the Solway – the Nith, the Annan, the Esk, the Eden, the Waver and the Wampool. All fishermen have to be licensed by a farmer or landowner whose land abuts on the rivers and the licence is only good for that property. Boundary disputes are not uncommon.

The Laird of Arbigland in Galloway, Captain Beauchamp Blackett, is a licenser and he introduced me to haaf netting.

It was a misty morning after a wet night as we tramped across the soggy sand flats below Carsethorn to the Nith. It was halfway of an ebb tide. Shrimp trawlers were churning up and down the Nith channel. The great sand flats of the Solway spread out before us, raucous with seabirds and with the green hills of Cumberland away to the south.

There were two haaf netters standing with the tide swirling around them. The great secret of haaf netting seems to be knowing where to stand for best. The channels change regularly as sand builds up in one place and is gouged out in another; this knowledge must be a combination of instinct, inherited savvy and observation. All these are important in a place of shifting sands, rip tides and sudden storms: the Solway takes lives every year.

As we watched, up went a net and the fisherman waded swiftly to the shore. Struggling in the folds was a nice sea trout (c. 3 lbs).

In the late afternoon we drove down the east bank of the Nith. Groups of men were assembling, waiting for the start of the flood tide. Here they worked in groups of five or six, lining out into the river, the outside man with water up to his chest. The tide was coming in at a great gallop and, as it rose, the outside man would move into the inshore end of the line. Step into a hole in a tide like that and the best you get will be a nasty fright. Nothing happened. All the fish were on the Cumberland side, it seemed, along with all the sand. The Solway is very fickle; some years it erodes the Scottish side and builds up England, other years it is vice versa; probably an English plot.

As we drove up the road towards Dumfries, the frantic squalls that had come driving out of the Galloway hills all day ceased. The sun came out, lighting up the river and the lines of haaf netters who were now spread up and down the lower reaches of the Nith. I wished them joy. I reckoned that haaf netting was a hard way to get a bit of fish for your tea.

[6]

To find Sandy Walker, you park opposite the pub, walk past the post office and turn into the yard with the red gates. At the back of the yard is a garage and if you go across to the north-east corner there is a wee door through which comes the strains of Radio Scotland Accordion Club, and there perched on his stool like a happy cherub is the great man himself.

Sandy is one of the last of the old village saddlers. He has plied his trade in the village of Milfield, Northumberland for forty years and is coming up eighty-two.

He was born in Lesmahagow where his father was a gamekeeper. He was first apprenticed to a saddler in 1927 and it has been his life. In 1934 he went to work for the CWS in Newcastle where the harness was made for all the Co-ops 'from Berwick to Land's End'. He stayed there for twenty years.

In 1954, Andrew Robinson retired from his saddler's business in Milfield and Sandy took over. There he is today, a supremely happy man who loves his work ('I've always enjoyed it; if I hadn't, I wouldn't be here') and is always happy to stop and have a 'bit of a crack' with a visitor.

His tiny workroom is piled high with saddles, harness, leather bags, gun cases and rolls of leather and canvas. Sandy seems to be able to stick his hand unerringly into the pile and pull out the particular item that is wanted. The view out of his only window is into a paddock full of ewes and lambs. The work bench under the window is a litter of tools, thread, leather strips and twine. Perched on his stool he sews and stitches and snips. His craftsmanship is a local legend and he will turn his hand to anything from making a leather bag, to stitching a saddle, to mending your shepherding shoes. He made me a Rolls-Royce of a roe sack, which I treasure.

But, then, Sandy is a treasure, within the meaning of the act, and a greatly respected man: thirty-three years a school governor and twenty-two years on the Parish Council. He is often called upon to give the toast of the 'Immortal Memory' at Burns Suppers. I once asked him if he played an instrument: 'Man, I couldn't play hell with a stick and a big drum.' He is a great admirer and quoter of Robert Burns: 'There'll never be another yin like him.' I think that his many friends would say the same about Sandy Walker.

NOTE Since that article appeared Sandy Walker has retired.

5. MORE CORPSE, MORE CLOTH

[1]

It is sad and melancholy that we seldom hear Grace said before a meal these days. It would do us no harm to remember that God was there before Tescos.

The Grace still in most general use is the good old 'For what we are about to receive, may the Lord make us truly thankful'. Quite right too; nothing wrong with that. It says it all, but what about a change on occasion? There are still a few educated padres who can trot out something pithy in Latin or Greek. It is sad that most of us are so classically challenged that we can do no more than look solemnly down our noses to see if decent-sized port glasses have been provided.

There are still a few old Graces in use in the Borders, which may be of use and interest. Try this one:

'Some hae meat and canna eat; some wad eat, but want it; we hae meat and we can eat, so let the Lord be thankit.' Then there is the slightly more earthy:

'Backs to the wall, Boys, bellies to the table; let's thank the Lord that we hae meat and eat whilst we are able.' The final one, for which I am indebted to Mr Hudson of Kensington, is probably of great antiquity:

'The Sheep of the Border: that claes oor backs and crams oor weam and may the shank bane of every sheep mak a whittle haft to cut the throats of our enemies wi'.' This one may just be a trifle lacking on the 'love thy neighbour' bit, but it does have a certain reeking robustness.

[2]

Leadenhall market has always fascinated me. As a spotty City clerk I used to wander there in my lunch hour amongst the rows of hanging game and poultry, admiring the great piles of fruit and veg and the marvellous displays of fish, before spending my luncheon voucher (half a crown/12.5p) on 'steak-a-pie and cheeps, 2 slices and a cuppa tea'.

The market on the field by the Leaden Hall was given its Charter by Dick Whittington who decreed that there should always be a fresh food market on the site.

Edward Blackett and his father, Captain Beauchamp Blackett, run Ashdowns (Leadenhall) Plc, one of the most famous fish shops in the City. This ties in nicely with their other interest, Beauchamps Restaurant, which provides quality nosh for the City quality.

4.30 am found me in the Ashdown van with Edward, heading
for Billingsgate Market. Billingsgate is a world on its own. It is a
noisy, fish-odorous place, awash with water, where you have to
be quick on your daisies (daisy roots – boots) if you do not want
to be run down by a barrow. Is it true about the robust language of
fish porters? yes. Fish comes from all over the world to Billingsgate:
brightly-coloured parrot fish flown in from Indonesia; sabre fish
from Senegal; Norwegian red fish; Montrose scallops; live eels
from New Zealand and did you know that Dover sole is the only
fish that you have to hang, like game? And did you also know that
Torbay sole is often sold as Dover sole? What is the difference?
about 2 quid.

Ashdowns opens at 0545. As soon as the fish arrived from
Billingsgate, Wally (fifty-five and in fish all his life) started building
up the amazing display of fish on the refrigerated slab. At the
back of the shop, Edward and Adam were setting up the orders for
the day: J. P. Morgan, Deutsche Bank, The Carpenters' Company,
Schroders . . . directors' dining-rooms and restaurants are the
backbone of Ashdowns' trade.

It was time for some welcome breakfast in the restaurant with
'The Captain' (as Capt. Blackett is universally referred to in the
Market): papaya, kippers, tea and lots of toast. Beauchamp's main
business is at luncheon.

Early workers were starting to thread their way through the
market. Many stopped to look at Wally's display. Mrs Adams
from Canning Town bought some skate: 'I do love the fish here;
it's lovely.'

With the Captain to W. Baxter and Son, Greengrocers. Mr
Leonard Baxter is the third generation in the shop. A tightly-curled
wrought-iron spiral staircase took us down into an Aladdin's cave
of a cellar. These cellars were part of the Roman Coliseum. Orders
from upstairs are lowered down on a bulldog clip and a piece of
string.

Outside the front of the shop is another artful display: carob nuts,
asparagus (English, Spanish and American); oyster mushrooms
from France; rambutans from Kenya; five kinds of peppers; Italian

radicchio; French artichokes; Spanish watermelons. Ninety per cent of Mr Baxter's trade is 'order', again mostly for directors' dining-rooms.

Our next call was to Robert Ashby Ltd – butchers and forty-three years in the Market. Patrick Thomas is the second generation in the shop. He buys only Scottish beef, direct from two main suppliers. The beasts are killed on a Friday and the beef arrives on the next Monday and is then hung for twelve days. Pork comes from Suffolk and the lamb is all organic; from Kent, Sussex or Devon. Mr Thomas also has a splendid selection of home-made sausages, salamis, home-cooked hams and cheeses. 'Benny' Benedicto is the resident cheese expert. Under his very sound advice, I took away some Farmhouse Caerphilly and some English Goat Cheese. Once more, Ashby's trade is 90 per cent with corporate customers.

When the Captain and I first knew Leadenhall, some thirty years ago, the Market was nearly all food shops: this is no longer the case, but one of the most famous survivors is the eponymous Butcher and Edmonds Ltd, with third generation Alan Butcher in command. Game is his great speciality and he sells all that he can get, mostly to the restaurant and dining-room trade. The game comes from dealers in Yorkshire, Durham and Norfolk. We both agreed that wild venison was best and roe doe the best of the best.

Below Ashdowns there is a cellar where the ice machines lurk and where there are huge tanks of running salt water with wriggling eels and peevish lobsters. Here the Captain, Edward and I picnicked. A dozen oysters makes a good start, then dressed crab, smoked eel, smoked salmon, brown bread and butter. There was a good, oaky Chardonnay to wash it all down and to propose a toast to the 'villagers' of Leadenhall who still provide first-class fresh food to the discriminating: I think that Dick Whittington would be proud of them.

[3]

They used to say that you could use 'every part of a pig, except its squeal'. Then they added, 'but now we can sell the squeal for use in the brakes of London taxis'. In the good/bad old days, most rural cottagers kept an annual pig. It was cosseted and pampered and fed on boiled up household scraps and garden waste mixed with a little meal. Then the pig killer cameth. The annual pig killing was a great neighbourhood occasion. The pig was stunned and then stuck, to bleed it. The carcase was scraped and scrubbed with boiling water. The offal went for immediate eating. The carcase was hung and then divided into shoulders, flanks and hams which would be salted, cured and hung in the kitchen for future consumption.

But what of the blood? did that just go down the drain? Heaven preserve your innocence. The blood was made into Black Puddings.

No one knows when 'blood puddings' were first made. Pigs are thought to have been first domesticated over 2,000 years ago and the invention of the black pudding cannot have been far behind. I would like to shake the hand of the inventor across the centuries: he was a great man. Blood puddings appear in various forms throughout Europe and Asia and amongst what we must now call 'Native Americans'. This ubiquity is not surprising since it is a delicious, nutritious and highly digestible food for which some claim aphrodisiac qualities or, as a rough friend of mine maintains, 'It puts a crack on you like a coachman's whip'.

What is black pudding? Some people are vague about it, including the MAFF who once decreed that it must have a 65% meat content, until it was pointed out that there was *no* meat in a *blood* pudding. The basic ingredients are pig's blood, cereal, fat and *seasoning*. I put seasoning in italic because it is this that makes the great differences in taste and flavour. Manufacturers guard the secrets of their seasoning with their lives. Most puddings are made by mixing the ingredients and then pouring them into an intestine.

You then have a sausage. This is barely simmered until cooked. The pudding can be eaten cold but is usually fried or grilled.

Black pudding is alive and well in Britain, but mainly in the north. Insipid southron (sic) palates cannot always rise to the challenge. It is still a most popular dish, as I discovered when I asked readers to recommend their favourites for a *Daily Telegraph* survey. The response was tremendous. Twenty-four butchers were recommended, of whom sixteen responded with samples.

Let me say at once that there are no losers in this survey. All the puddings tasted were delicious and all quite distinctive. All and any will provide a culinary delight for readers. But there has to be a winner and in the end it is all a matter of personal preference. The three finalists were Thornley ('Firm, very fine delicate flavour'), Husband and Wife ('Firm, spicy, great flavour') and Higginsons ('Sturdy, tremendous burst of flavour'). The final took place one breakfast time, Chez Poole: those present – Self, Wife and the Boy. The opinion split three ways but, as Chairman, I gave my casting vote to Higginsons (dammit! am I not master in my own house?).

Higginsons (a member of the prestigious 'Q Guild' of butchers) is very much a family business with Stewart and his wife Pauline and Stewart's mother, Jessie. Their pride in their work shines out of their happy faces and the wonderful display of food in the shop (always crowded). But Jessie is our heroine, because she is the pudding maker. She comes from a long line of Yorkshire farmers and pork butchers. I watched her at work.

These days the pigs' blood comes in powdered form. Jessie just adds cold water and makes a slurpy black porridge, to which is added soaked and boiled groats (husked oats). Next comes liquidised raw vegetables (onions and celery are very important) and the secret, secret herb mixture – 'a handful of this, a handful of that. I never weigh'. Then there is the chopped and blanched pork back fat and it must be *back* fat. It is mixed by hand ('She's a bit rough and ready,' says Stewart, 'she slaps it about'). The mixture has to be even. As Jessie mixes, the most tantalising aroma starts to tingle the nose. The mixture is then handed into baking trays. This is one (maybe crucial) difference between the Higginson puddings and most others – they are baked. The pudding is patted down and covered in foil, then put into a medium oven (180°C/350°F/gas mark 4) for 1 hour and 10 minutes. Then there it is, looking like a great slab of delicious fruit cake, although it is in fact an absolutely delicious Black Pudding – enjoy!

NOTE I wish I could give the names and addresses of all twenty-four butchers who took part in the survey, but that would not be practical. However, *see* the Appendix for details of the three finalists.

[4]

There was a dread rumour going about that British Rail was giving up serving kippers for breakfast. Now, I love kippers, even if they do lead to discreet fish-laden belching, but they have become difficult to find. I remember ordering kippers in Stornoway with eager anticipation. The thing that came looked like a poor little butterfly. The herrings had gone, said the waitress sadly: no herrings – no kippers.

I am happy to say that the kipper is with us yet and so is the BR kipper. They serve 70,000 per annum on Intercity trains. The Savoy Hotel serves 800 lbs of kippers yearly and the demand remains constant. But where to find good kippers – plump, juicy kippers, properly smoked and with no nasty dyes added for the colouring? I lifted up my nose and whiffled for that unique salty, tangy, smoky smell. My nose lead me to Seahouses on the Northumberland coast.

Seahouses used to be one of the great herring ports. Older people can remember being able to walk across the harbour on the moored boats. Every year, in the summer, the herring drifters used to follow the 'Silver Darlings' up the east coast. The sea-borne migration would be matched on land by the fisher girls, who would move from port to port. You can see the old photographs of them in their long skirts and poke bonnets as they laboured away, gutting and salting huge piles of herrings and packing them into mountains of wooden casks – hardy women. There are now only about a dozen boats operating out of Seahouses and their future may be sadly small – like the North Sea herrings. A lot of herrings come from Iceland now.

South Street, with the harbour at its foot, was once the street of the herring and that is where my nose led me to Swallow Fish Ltd – proprietors John and Pauline Swallow. John Swallow is a character. He was born in Seahouses. His father was in the oil business, but John did not take to it. He went dairy farming in Lincolnshire. Then he went to the fishing off western Scotland, sailing out of Mallaig. Twenty years ago he came back to Seahouses and opened his shop and smokery in South Street. He owns bumpy South Street. The Council offered to take it over but, as he says, the first thing they would have done would have been to paint yellow lines. South Street remains private, bumpy, parkable and redolent of kippers.

It is thought that the kipper may have originated in Seahouses. Legend has it that c.1840 one John Woodge had hung some herrings in his 'guffy sty' to dry. The sty burned down and the first herrings were kippered. 'Guffy'? Fishermen never say the word P-I-G – it is unlucky, although if you grasp cold steel the bad luck is negated. Likewise, seeing a clergyman or a blonde woman on the way to your boat might make you turn round and go home.

Before you kipper a herring, it has to be split and gutted and here things have changed. There is a machine – an amazing, Emmett-like construction of wheels, levers and clanking cogs that looks big enough to split a whale. This machine can handle 60 stone (and you can metricate that for yourselves – do you good) per hour. The herrings are placed on a circular turntable that feeds them into this mechanical Moloch. They emerge, neatly split, from one shoot and the guts come out of another. The fish are then immersed in a 60% brine solution for about fifteen minutes. They are then hooked on a rack ready for the smoking.

The king of the smokehouse is Patrick Wilkin; he started working with John whilst he was still at school, and he is a man in love with his work.

The smokehouse reaches the height of the building, its walls blackened and tarred with years of smoke. Up in the rafters hang rack upon rack of herrings and salmon. Salmon take forty-eight hours to smoke, herring eleven. Six piles of hardwood (oak is best) shavings are put on the floor and topped off with sawdust to make smoke. The first fire is lit at 0400 and the last at 1800, but Patrick often pops down in the evening to top up the fires.

John showed me the old stables at the back where he used to have a high-density mussel purification plant. The mussel trade used to give employment to six men, but Brussels put a stop to that. The old wood and metal mussel trays that had done well for years had to go. It would have cost £70,000 to meet EC regulations. That side of the business was closed down. John and I feel the same way about EC regs. Did you know that a fishing boat, even a day boat, has to carry 150 condoms? Still, I suppose that they come in handy if you cut a finger. We talked of the total disregard of other EC countries for catch quotas and net sizes. It is worth noting that Spain is reputed to have five fishery inspectors, all based in salty maritime Madrid. The UK has 142 at the ports and twenty-six more at HQ.

The shop was continuously full of customers, which was not surprising when you saw the goodies on display. The shop also has a display of coopering tools and a fascinating gallery of old photographs of the boom days of the herring fishing.

As I left with a stone of kippers tucked under my arm (you can get them by post, *see* Appendix) the smoke was pouring from the smokehouse vents, its oaky smeech mingling with the smell of the sea coming up from the harbour.

I had two lovely, fat, juicy, tasty kippers for my luncheon and belched happily all afternoon. Kippers are alive and well and living in Seahouses.

[5]

'Well, there's Kingston Blacks, Coalbrooks, Tom Potts, Morgan Sweet, Sheep's Noses, Billy Down Pippins and buggered if I knaw what else. Kingston Blacks is the best apple, but you've got to have a mix.' Reg Snell and Peter Hansford are talking Cider Apples.

In the West Country, cider is not just a drink, it is part of a way of life.

Reg's cider house is attached to the shippen (cow shed). Against the wall is a row of cobwebbed barrels – some empty and waiting, some with last year's cider in, a pale amber liquid, sharp and clean on the palate.

Brooding at the back of the shed is the press – a square wooden platform and above it a mighty oaken beam of great age (how old? 'Bliddy sight older 'n I') with two mighty iron screws running through it. In the foreground is the mill – a purpose-built machine from Dennings of Chard c. 1920. The mill is belt-driven from the PTO of a tractor – 'Er's a stationary engine, because er's got a flat tyre.'

The apples are poured into the top of the mill, a torrent of red, green and yellow. Apples need to be ripe (some say rotten) to make cider; they are picked up off the ground – 'a bit of sheep shit adds to the flavour'. In the mill, they are first crunched by the 'clappers' and then ground some more between two granite rollers. The mush that comes out of the bottom is called 'pummy'.

A square frame is laid on the bed of the press and hessian sacking is laid out on the frame. The pummy is shovelled from the bottom of the mill onto the sacking. There it is spread by hand and the frame is gradually raised, bringing the cloth with it. Then the frame is removed and the sacking is folded over the pummy like a parcel – this is a 'cake'. It takes six bags of apples to make one cake.

Six cakes are built up one on top of the other – this equals a 'cheese'. One cheese = two hogsheads (108 gallons) of cider and two hogsheads = one butt. Why is it called a cheese? 'I hant got no idea, really. When I were a tacker [youth] 'twere always called a cider cheese' – so that is an end to the matter.

When the cheese is ready, a heavy board is placed on top of it and the massive beam is screwed down onto the board. The juice is already starting to flow.

Opinions differ about the pressing. Peter Hansford, who makes cider at Dowlish Wake, goes for a maximum press on the first night with a further pressing the next day. But Peter has a much more modern mill (he can make a cheese in twenty minutes) that grinds exceeding small. Reg Snell's ageing mill produces a much coarser pummy that has to be pressed gradually. It takes him over an hour to set up the cheese which is then pressed gradually over two days. The pummy is then taken out and the cakes remade and pressed again. The discarded pummy is then fed to the cows – cows love it.

With the Snell cheese taking the first gentle pressure and the honey-coloured liquid starting to pour through the strainer into the vat, it is time for supper. A straw bale is ceremoniously covered with a cloth to make a table. Other bales and old fuel drums are arranged as seats. Out come wonderful cottage loaves, a prime piece of Stilton and some good sweet onions – 'Now what do 'ee want better'n that?' And to drink? 'Well, what do 'ee think?' Cider, of course.

So we sit and munch ('That's what I call a bit of Stilton, makes the roof of your mouth sting') and slurp whilst the yarns go round and round. The talk is of cows and hay ('Three pound a bliddy bale 'tis fetching now') and hunting and who is doing what to whom. Then the singing starts – 'Drink up thee cider, drink up thee cider . . .'

All the time the juice trickles into the vat. This is pure apple juice which tastes honey sweet. The juice is strained and put in the barrel. After two days it starts to ferment ('working'). You cannot make cider with peeled apples, the skins are vital for the fermentation.

Is anything put into the cider? Some people put a bit of steak in, sultanas, oranges, beetroot, and if you make cider in a rum barrel, then look out – that is Fighting Cider. You would 'fall out with the stones in a wall'.

'. . . for the carn's [sic] half cut and so be we and so be weeee!'

So when can you drink the cider? it may be up to six months and certainly not before Christmas. 'Drink er too much before that and you need a wisp of hay in your pocket to go home with'; 'Apple juice won't hurt 'ee, but if you drink er when er's working, er'll work you.'

I'll tell 'ee what, My Handsome, the bugger worked me all through thic night.

NOTE It is er not 'er – er is the old Saxon word for 'it' – not a lot of people know that.

[6]

'Why don't you learn to carve?': a petulant female cry heard in thousands of domestic dining-rooms and kitchens. Carving meat is a thing that men are supposed to know about. These days few of them seem to be able to manage more than a heap of mangled chunks. I went to consult the experts at that great temple of traditional flesh eating: Simpson's-in-the-Strand in London. You do not dress just any old how for carving at Simpson's: you need an apron, a chef's hat and a white coat. Simpson's do not have coats for a 52-inch chest.

First to the kitchens where 'Master Cook', Tony Bradley, produced a 3-lb. side of smoked salmon to be sacrificed in the cause. In any carving, the knife is of vital importance and it has to be SHARP and kept SHARP with judicious use of oil stone and steel.

For smoked salmon, Tony likes a serrated blade, c. 12 inches long. Start at the tail end of the side and carve from the head towards the tail with the knife at a slight angle so that it follows the grain of the flesh. This should produce large, wide, thin slices. Resist the urge to clench the knife in a terror-stricken grip. Just relax. Make the knife an extension of your arm and then let the knife do the work, just sliding through the firm orange flesh, with the full length of the blade coming into play. You begin to realise that carving is a thoroughly satisfying and pleasurable business. From a side of this size, Tony would expect to carve 10–12 portions: my score? about 8–9. Verdict? not bad at all.

Beef and lamb are the heart of Simpson's. As part of the Savoy Group all their meat is bought by the great Mr Swann. Mr Swann's only orders are to buy the best. He has no budget, but spends about £1.5 million per annum. The huge, mouth-watering sirloins laid out for inspection were all Aberdeen Angus. The flesh was dark red as a result of two–three weeks' hanging, with a fine layer of thick creamy textured fat and good marbling. This is how proper British beef should look; quite unlike that ghastly, bright red, unhung, tasteless stuff that supermarkets foist upon the ignorant.

Three silver-domed trolleys awaited me in the South Room along with Brian Clivaz, the General Manager, Donal MacAuley, Assistant Manager, and John Cockerill, twenty years a carver at Simpson's and a man in love with carving. We started with the beef.

Beef is best carved in the 'traditional English way': that is, thin slices to bring out the full flavour and texture. No, you do not just chop down into the beef; you carve on a gentle slant. Once again, do not force the knife, let it work for you, keep the knife flat and just let it slide down through the beautiful grain of the beef to the bone; shift your fork to the top of the slice, lay the slice across your knife and present for the approbation of the client before putting it on the plate. John uses a 'Beef Carving Knife' with a rounded end. Carving a good sirloin, he says, is 'something so pleasant that sometimes you never want to stop'. It *is* most satisfying. John's 'You've done very well with the beef' was as welcome as the huge glass of sherry that Mr Clivaz conjured up.

Next came a saddle of lamb. Make an initial cut straight down one side of the back bone, then slide the knife underneath to loosen the meat from the ribs. Cut across the saddle at the line where the loin meets the chump. Carve two lengthways strips about ¼ inch thick from the loin. Put the knife under the joint and turn it over to reveal the fillet and remove two nice large slices. Turn the joint over again and perhaps Sir would like a nice slice off the chump? There is your Simpson's portion neatly arranged on the plate (always with the fat away from the customer). For this job you need a 'French Carver': a stiff-bladed knife (SHARP) with a point. You should get eight such portions off a saddle. My performance was 'not bad at all'.

The pheasant is trickier. You need a small, pointed, stiff-bladed knife – and a pause for more sherry. Then lick your moustache, turn the pheasant on its side and cut in behind the wing bone. Now lift the leg away from the body and snap it back to pull the bone out of the socket; slice through. Now find (with some difficulty) the elbow joint and cut through that. Hold the bird upright with your fork on one side of the breast and carve three–four nice slices off the opposite breast. That is the theory: my practice? 'One lump, or two, sir?'

There can be no nicer way to end the course than to see the whole thing done properly from the receiving end over luncheon. Do not forget the fine old custom of tipping the carver: that will be obligatory in my house from now on.

[7]

Richard Paterson has a very expensive nose. No, not *that* sort of nose. Mr Paterson's nose is expensive because it must be one of the most sensitive and skilled olfactory organs in the business

– the business being whisky blending. Mr Paterson is the Master Blender for the Whyte and Mackay Group and therefore the very man to discuss my problem with.

I am very fond of whisky. For moments of special relaxation, I like a single malt. A parenthesis: readers confused by whisky terminology should try an excellent little booklet *Scotch Whisky – questions and answers* published by the Scotch Whisky Association, Edinburgh (*see* Appendix). Of the single malts, I love those of Islay best – especially Laphroaig and Lagavulin with their wonderful evocations of seaweed, tar, salt and peat. For everyday drinking I prefer a blended whisky and, for choice, The Buchanan – 8 years old. This is the problem: The Buchanan is not available at the moment and when present stocks run out, I shall be bereft of my favourite whisky. Could Mr Paterson blend a whisky which would suit my taste?

The blending room at Whyte and Mackay's headquarters in Glasgow is light and white and clinically clean. The glass cupboards around the walls carry row upon row of famous whiskies, some of them historic. Whisky is historic. The name 'whisky' derives from the Gaelic '*Uisge Beatha*' – water of life. Whisky is probably as old as cultivated barley, but its first recorded mention was in the Scottish Exchequer Rolls of 1494, so it is officially five hundred years old.

Richard Paterson is a dapper moustached man in his forties. He is in love with whisky and it is bred in him. Both his father and grandmother were whisky blenders. He explained that it can take years to produce a new blend for the market and in my case there was only one evening to work in. However, as he knew of my taste for Islay malts and The Buchanan, he felt that this gave him a good enough base to work on in the time available.

A blend is a mixture of grain and malt whiskies and up to fifty different whiskies may go to make a single blend. Mr Paterson explained that blending whisky is like planning a party – you invite people who you hope will get on together, but who will each contribute an individual something to make the thing go with a swing. But you have to be careful about inviting the Islay boys:

'They are the hard men of whisky and if you are not careful they can take over the place.' To stop the 'big' malts smashing the furniture, you have to mix them with more gentle, 'feminine' whiskies who will 'seduce them' and calm them down.

Richard (whisky breaks down formality) had assembled ten whiskies to be nosed and blended.

Sample 1 – Invergordon Grain 1971 – a light, flowery whisky which told you that it had been matured in a bourbon cask (that is an oak cask that had originally carried Bourbon whiskey – the Americans and the Irish add an e).

Sample 2 was North of Scotland (distillery now closed) Grain 1972 – soft, sweet and delicate – we definitely want her at the party.

Sample 3 was North British 1971 – full and rich and with good body. Why *Hello*!

'These are three exciting females. They are going to seduce people and bring style and elegance to the party' – whey heh heh!

Sample 4 was Glenkinchie Lowland Malt 1982 – light, fragrant and feminine. Oh yes please!

Sample 5: Glen Albyn (distillery closed) Highland Malt 1971 – full and redolent of sherry cask. Looks game.

Sample 6: Longmorn 1973 – heavy yet delicate, again with a hint of sherry. A jolly nice sort.

Sample 7: Fettercairn Highland Malt 1976 – think of melons and rejoice.

Sample 8: Glen Scotia Cambeltown Malt 1972 – rich and refined with hidden complexities. The party is shaping well.

Sample 9: Bruichladdich 1969 – peaty, muscular and lusty as a sailor. The Islay lads have arrived and the decibel level is definitely rising.

Sample 10: Scapa 35-Year-Old – complex and takes time to come across, but when it does . . .

The party was now complete. All the guests were then assembled in a mixing jar and left to get in the party spirit. In the meantime, Richard introduced me to some real aristocrats of the house – Whyte & Mackay Special Reserve – round and mellow; Whyte and Mackay 21-Year-Old Blend – full flavoured and goes on and on and on; Whyte and Mackay 30-Year-Old Blend – distinguished and floral with a hint of wood; and 500th Anniversary Blend – elegant, distinguished and long matured in Oloroso casks. Then Richard produced a small labelled flask from a cupboard: 'Take a sip. Now roll it round your mouth. Now hold it. Now swallow. I am going to count down – 10 . . . Zero!' Spot on the zero came the sensory equivalent of a nuclear explosion with after-shocks all through the system. Did I like it? yes! yes! YES! What on earth was it? 'Very few people have ever drunk that.' 'That' was a 1926 Dalmore Malt. It sells at £4,000 (yes, thousand) per bottle. Most purchasers put it unopened in the bank. Well, whatever turns you on, but I shall never forget our all too brief coupling.

As I write, I have a glass of my special blend at my elbow and it bears a remarkable and happy similarity to The Buchanan, but it must have a name. I consulted a friend who has the Gaelic. He came up with '*Liam Mhorgneasach* (vorgnaysock)' – Big William's Whisky. He also suggested a toast: '*Scaoil amach an bobailin*', but, knowing my friend's sense of humour, I will just say, '*Slainte*' (Good Health).

NOTE Regretfully, The Buchanan is still 'resting'.

[8]

'I'M NOT FAT!'

Dr Burgess studied me silently over his half-moon spectacles and I could see another fiver going on the bill. He then reached out a finger and prodded. The great balloon of skin round my middle wobbled and I hung my head in shame. It is hard to be dignified with nothing but your socks on, as any of those Swedish movies will demonstrate. I had just tipped the scales at 19 stone

10 lbs (276 lbs) and if you want it in metric then you can do it yourself. I was fat.

'You've got to lose a stone and I mean it. At least a stone. You are grossly overweight.'

I WAS FAT. No man can deceive his belt. I have worn the same belt for some years and over those years the outward progression from hole to hole has marked my descent into 'age, vice and unsoundness'. To ram the truth home I had just had all my suits let out: 'Getting quite like Mr X (a well-known and genial junior minister), sir,' said Derek as he cheerfully plied his tape measure. 'We like our gentlemen to grow: more corpse, more cloth.'

I did not like growing, but the problem was (and is) that I love food and am desperately greedy. That night I picked at my food, refused seconds and nibbled some dry toast. 'What can ail him?' cried my genial hostess. 'He is pecking at my lovely food like a spuggy.' So the whole sad story came out and the assembled company dabbed its collective eye. Then a Lloyds broker said, 'What you need is the hay diet.'

I mulled this over and, being properly suspicious of advice offered by Lloyds brokers, asked whether he had Meadow Hay or Rye Grass Hay in mind and please could I be excused silage. This rather threw the urban company, but making allowances for a slow-thinking bucolic, it explained that the Hay Diet had nothing to do with hay ('You are an old silly') and everything to do with Dr Hay, an American doctor, who had invented the thing some fifty years ago. I said that I would give it a bash.

There are numerous books about the Hay Diet which you may devour at your leisure. It is sufficient to say that it is not so much a diet as a way of life. The basis of it is that you eat in a way that your digestion was designed to cope with. A lot of obesity problems are caused by overloading the system. The digestion cannot cope properly with the overload and solves the problem by shunting off the excess into a siding where it sits and gradually turns into unwanted fat.

The important basic principle of the Hay Diet is that you do not combine Protein and Carbohydrates; this is what makes the digestive system throw a wobbly. Thus, you may eat Fish *or* Chips, but not Fish *and* Chips: you may eat Roast Beef *or* Roast Potatoes, but you should not mix them. Sweets, cakes, pies and suchlike lovely rubbish you must consign to the dustbin of memory. One of the plus points of the Hay Diet is that it makes no mention of alcohol and I have never been fool enough to ask.

On the next morning I breakfasted with Mr Bentley, the General Manager of Claridges. I ordered fruit salad. Mr Bentley studied me severely over his spectacles and suggested that some eggs, some fried bread, some kidneys, some . . . I explained about the diet. A slight spasm of pain crossed his face, before his training reasserted itself and he ordered a large plate of fruit salad for Mr Poole.

The first month was the worst. I yearned for incorrect combinations. The sight of a fish and chip shop gave me palpitations. I learned to stave off the pangs by eating fruit between meals: you should not eat it with meals, because the system does not approve.

My wife, God bless her, entered into the spirit of things and also joined the Hay Gang, although she has little obvious need for a diet. She bought a vegetarian cookbook, as her wondrous pies were now on the forbidden list. I am a great lover of the potato: Vegetable Shepherds Pie is now high on the list of favourites. We occasionally dine on just potatoes (in various forms) and salad or vegetables. Sunday is Sin Day when the diet declares a Non Dies and when I can gorge myself on meat *and* spuds *and* have a pudding.

After six weeks the initial agony had abated somewhat and I had lost a stone in weight.

Hooray! you might think: now our hero can return to his old unreconstructed ways! Not so. The fact was that not only had I lost weight, but I felt very much better, both physically and mentally. All in the mind? What is not? '*Mens sana in corpore sano*' tells it like it is.

'Diet', in the sense of something to lose weight by, is really a misnomer when it comes to the Hay Diet. Dr Hay wanted his regime to become a way of life and a whole new way of eating.

In fact, it is a very old way of eating. The good Doctor based it on the eating habits of primitive hunter gatherers who ate what they had hunted or gathered, but seldom mixed the ingredients. The mixing is a gluttonous habit brought about by those who began living to eat instead of eating to live. The weight loss brought about by the Hay Diet is a side-show. Indeed, you are told to stop worrying about weight. Stick to the diet and you will adjust your weight naturally.

The Hay Diet is now part of my life. I do not bang on about it (much) but people started getting at me: 'You've lost so much weight!', 'Your clothes are hanging off you.' I had to punch some inward holes in my belt; we were on unknown territory. My agent said that she hoped that I was not going to become 'lean and sardonic'; fat authors are apparently more biddable.

I knew that I was really getting somewhere when the incomparable Mr Maresca of the Savoy Grill started expressing concern about my thinness, 'but you love your food so much!' as indeed I do. I have declared the Grill a Non-Diet Area; just to please Mr Maresca, you understand.

There the matter rests, or rather does not. I am still losing weight, albeit not with the original rush. The spare tyre has largely gone. I feel hugely better. My tailor has demanded the right to take all my suits in again. As I write this, just six months into the Hay Diet, I have lost 30 lbs weight.

Thank you, Dr Hay.

6. SUMMER

[1]

At the time of writing the may blossom is at its peak. I always look forward to its heady scent; it is the nearest thing to the scent of orange blossom that we get in England. At the same time, the whins and the broom are in full flower, spreading streaks of gold across green banks and hillsides.

Driving through the lanes the other morning in the warm darkness of the pre-dawn, I had my window wound down and the van filled with the scent of thorn, gorse, broom and cow parsley. Coming home later, when the sun was up, the ungrazed meadows produced a pot-pourri of scent from the cow parsley, with buttercups, clover, shepherd's purse and I do not know what else added in.

When the grass is cut for hay, there will be the wonderful smell of sun-baked grass and herbs; this is one of the most evocative smells I know, as it comes wafting through the windows of an evening. Well-made and properly baled hay encapsulates this smell so that when you open a bale on some dark January morning, there is a sudden fleeting whiff of the scents of summer.

Just in case you think I am waxing a bit lyrical, there are other scents of summer: there is the compacted litter from the sheep shed to be mucked out and the dip to be cleaned out after several hundred sheep have been through it: that brings the nose out of the air. Then there is something very dead in one of the broom thickets. The sickly smell of decomposition mingles with the scent of the flowers and encourages one to philosophise on life and death.

The hedges on the farm are very old. They almost certainly date back to the Enclosure Acts which would make them at least 150 years old. They were not well maintained in the past and some of them have been reduced to a line of scattered thorn trees stitched together with modern high-tensile sheep fencing. But these old bushy trees have their own charm with their fantastically writhen and twisted trunks, the bottom parts of which are polished by the rubbing of generations of sheep and cattle.

One of the trees blew down in a recent gale. Fred was itching to get the chain saw at it and 'tidy it up'. But there are still roots in the ground and the tree is still alive and well, so there it stays; it is good shelter for lambs.

Some of the hedges are still more or less intact, especially on the roadside where steel netting has prevented too much ovine depredation. Every year the contractor used to come with his tractor-mounted machine and trim them into neat, tidy box-like shapes. About three years ago, I stopped this. Neatness is not all, I decided, let the hedges grow free. This fit of bad husbandry has been rewarded this year. The roadside is a blaze, a splash, a great broad brush stroke of wild roses – pink and white and mixed. Every morning when I do my early round of the stock, I ride very slowly down the length of this hedge feeding on this sight whilst it lasts. The roses are now at their peak and will soon be gone, but what a feast. I am all for tidy farming, but sometimes a bit of scruffiness can be very rewarding.

[2]

To the Three Counties Show, at Malvern, in sackcloth and ashes (so fetching, my dears): I had a penance to make. Some time ago I wrote that the only beef worth eating was that which comes from Aberdeen Angus and Hereford beasts. I then received a monumental rocket from Albert Beer (the Secretary of the Devon Cattle Breeders Society) pointing out that a good old West Country boy like me should know better, especially me that was brought up with South Devons and all, and I should be ashamed of myself: so I was.

Devons are one of the oldest British breeds. They are docile, hardy and very adaptable, which is why they are exported to eighteen overseas countries. They are very good at converting grass into first-class beef, beef that has the 'marbling' of intramuscular fat so important for the cooking. Now I know that someone is going to point out that fewer people are having a proper Sunday joint these days. My reply is that this is mostly because people are too idle to cook properly. Someone will also say that fewer people are eating red meat: more fool them. It is small wonder that we are becoming a nation of whingeing wimps who lose at everything we do. A diet of convenience foods makes people too weak in mind and body to do anything.

There is nothing like a good bit of beef to fettle a chap and that was why I was at the Three Counties. The Devon Breeders had agreed to forgive me and to present me with a joint of beef. So there I was in the cattle lines posing with Atlantic Demand, the Champion bull from the Bowldown Herd, and Martin Gibson, the Bowldown Herdsman for twenty-three years, whilst John Lee (President of the Devon Cattle Breeders) presented me with a splendid piece of topside. Cameras clicked and flashed, the crowd oohed! and aaahed! and wondered which was better looking: me or Atlantic Demand. A little girl said that she liked the one with horns the best and I nearly said . . . but I didn't. Then we all went and had a drink.

[3]

I have a new cock (oh dear! oh dear! how your mind works). I have kept game fowl for some thirty years and I needed a change of blood. The new cock is a very handsome fellow and has been about his business to the extent that we now have three broods of chicks and another hen sitting. Game hens are mistresses at hiding their nests and sometimes the first we know is when the proud (and fierce) mother produces her cheeping brood in public.

Sometimes secrecy is their undoing, like the old besom who hatched a brood in the bottom of a huge wooden chest that had once been used for horse feed and had become a repository for everything from electric fencing posts to rusty axes. Of course, the hen could get out, but the chicks could not. It was very lucky that we found them in time.

It occurs to me that many people will never have seen a hen clucking about with her brood – little fluffy balls milling around her feet with bewildering speed and racing to the special sound that means she has scratched up a dainty morsel from the muck heap. As I watched the chicks I thought of the lady who told me that meat was murder and that she only eats eggs. Those chicks were eggs. I hope that she feels like a murderess.

★   ★   ★

This seems a good moment for a cock story. There was a retired shepherd who was living in peace with his pension, his garden and a few hens who scratched about under the watchful eye of Major, the cock. Major liked to celebrate the coming of dawn with a good solid crowing session. The young couple who moved into the cottage next door were 'Incomers' – wide eyed and eager in their search for rural tranquillity, 'getting their heads together' and generally plugging their vibes into Mother Nature. However, they soon found that Major's vocal triumphalism at the first seeping of the dawnlight was un-cool, un-tranquil and generally spaced them out (or something like that).

They took themselves next door as a deputation of complaint – something had to be done about Major's crowing, how else could they sleep to their customary 10 o'clock and gather the necessary strength to go and cash their Giro?

The old man listened to this tirade in silence. Then, still without saying a word, he caught Major, wrung his neck and handed the still twitching mortal husk to the horrified couple, who blurted out that they had had something less terminal in mind.

'Well,' said the old man, 'you can have a crowing cock, or a dead cock, but there ain't nothing in between.'

[4]

Most sheep shearing today is done by machine and usually by contractors. A lot of the contractors are local people, but there are gangs of shearers (usually Antipodean) who spend their year travelling the world, following the summer. In my part of the world, shearing is called 'clipping' and usually happens about the middle of June. One is entitled to expect that some signs of summer might be appearing by then and, if the Clerk of the Weather does happen to read this piece, would he please extract his digit and do something about it. I am very surprised that the

EC has not landed some inch-thick form on us: as it might be 'Weather Administration and Nature Control System'. To clip before June would allow the freezing Northumbrian spring breezes to play round the udders of the lactating ewes and would invite 'udder clap' (or mastitis, if you prefer). To clip much later would mean the ewes suffering heat stress and fly strike.

Most shearers love their work and it is certainly highly skilled. A skilled man can do c. 300 sheep a day. I think the charge is about £1 per sheep. It is indeed sweaty labour and they earn every penny that they make. I tried to learn once many years ago, but could not gaffer it: too much bending for a back that had started to remember a lot of hunting falls. The experts tell me that it is a job that you have to become accustomed to early in life, so that your back gets tuned in as it were.

You would think that, with all this mechanisation, the old hand shears would have become a curiosity, confined to farming museums or the smarter sort of potting shed; in fact, they are alive and well. Every shepherd will have a pair in his bag. They will be used for jobs such as 'cowing' (removing the soiled wool from the nether regions of a sheep), trimming off wool to treat things like blow fly strike (not a job for the squeamish) and sometimes out on the hill there will be that cunning old bitch who managed to evade the clipping gathering: she can be caught up and given the tonsorial treatment.

I was amazed to read that there are still more than sixty different patterns of hand shears being made. They are hand made from high carbon steel. To the best of my knowledge and belief the only remaining manufacturer in this country is Burgeon and Ball of Sheffield whose shears are exported all over the world. It seems that hand shearing is considered beneficial and cost effective in hotter climates and a good hand shearer can do 200 sheep a day: not as much as a mechanised shearer, you might say, but towards the end of the last century a man called Jack Howe sheared 320 sheep in less than eight hours. Now that is going some; his back must indeed have been sprung like Sheffield steel.

*   *   *

Roy came to clip his sheep that are running on one of my grass parks. Whilst he was here I got him to clip the three Scotch Blackface wethers that are growing quietly into mutton in the Home Field. We had some home-grown mutton for luncheon last Sunday and it was delicious, much to be preferred to the blander taste (or total lack of taste) in so much of the lamb that is sold these days. Very few butchers bother to hang their meat properly any more. It is more expensive for them to do so and if the public is not bothered by tasteless meat, why should they be? Well-hung mutton is a pleasure that few people enjoy these days. Have you ever tried asking for it at the butchers? most of them would give you the bum's rush. It is only at butchers who cater for the Asian citizens that you can buy mutton and this would mostly be from old draft ewes and destined for curry. Three-year-old wether mutton is almost impossible to find and that is why I grow my own.

But I digress, I digress; the ramblings of an old man, you understand; I really wanted to talk about wool. I gave Roy the three fleeces as payment for the clipping and I strongly suspect that he lost out on the deal. As I understand the current situation, the value of a fleece hardly pays for the cost of clipping it, let alone the costs of labour involved in gathering the sheep and rolling and packing the fleeces. If it were not for the fact that removing the fleece is important for the health and comfort of the sheep in the warm summer weather (wherever that may be) which brings the blow fly and the maggots, the game would hardly be worth the candle. The sad fact is that there is a world-wide glut of wool, with huge stock piles of the stuff. You probably would not think this if you go to buy a woollen garment. Whoever's pocket you may be lining when you buy that sweet, but terribly expensive new cardy, it is not the pocket of the poor old primary producer.

★

[5]

The Berkeleys of that Ilk came over with William the Conqueror and did pretty well for themselves – if we gloss over what was done to Edward II in the dungeons of Berkeley Castle. At one time, the Berkeleys could hunt from Charing Cross to the Severn on their own land, their servants wearing the yellow livery which is still worn by Berkeley Hunt servants to this day. 'Berkeley Hunt' even went into cockney rhyming slang – so next time you call someone a 'Berk' you will actually know what it means.

Some time in the reign of Henry I, a Berkeley had 'a little woman trouble at court' and moved as far north as he could to the Stonehaven area. Here the family became Barclay, bold and bad – they boiled the Provost of Aberdeen for being importunate in his demands for taxes, an idea that might concentrate the bureaucratic mind quite wonderfully. A Barclay went to Russia as a mercenary and in 1814 rode into Paris at the head of 100,000 Cossacks. This is the furthest west any Russian Army has been and remember a Brit got it there.

The Barclays then became bankers, Quakers and helped free the slaves. It was an obvious progression from there to becoming farmers and foxhunters and pillars of the C of E. This year is the centenary of the Barclay mastership of the Puckeridge Hounds in Hertfordshire – four generations. 'The Captain', as Captain Charles Barclay is generally known, is now the head of the Clan; he became joint master in 1947, a position he still retains with his daughter and one of his three sons.

Country people like stability and continuity – the Barclay family supply both, together with the benign autocracy, which works so much better in hunting than bad democracy. It is not just in the foxhunting world where the Captain is a much respected elder statesman – the Brent Pelham estate is a shining example of good environmental practice, allied with sound farming. Hedgerows have not been grubbed out. Copses are properly maintained. It was nice to return to the old mellow red-bricked hall after ten years and see that little has changed – except for a new stair carpet.

The Captain had invited me to help judge the Centenary Puppy Show (more correctly – Judging of the Young Hounds). Foxhound puppies are usually whelped at the kennels. Aged ten to twelve weeks they go out 'to walk' at farms and private houses where they can have the freedom to develop their bodies and minds and learn that chasing chickens gets you a smacked bottom. By the time they are a year old, they go back to the kennels to start their further education. This leads them up to the start of their hunting career (at c. 18 months of age) in the following autumn.

During the summer a show is held where the young hounds are judged by a pair of visiting masters and prizes are distributed to the Puppy Walkers – it is a great rural social occasion. A Centenary Puppy Show is an even greater occasion. Captain Barclay is an old friend, but I was very flattered to be asked to judge – after all, I am not even an MFH any more. My co-judge was to be the great Major John Berkeley of Berkeley Castle and long-time master and owner of the eponymous hounds.

It was a tremendous occasion. They sat down over 400 people to luncheon in a large marquee. It was a wonderful traditional English gathering and celebration. It was even traditional enough to tip down with rain throughout the judging of the Young Hounds. The only break with tradition was that the Captain provided a steel band to entertain the guests at luncheon and I did feel sorry for the unfortunate judge (I wonder which one) who was ordered to get up and sing calypsos with the band, but that is your benign autocracy for you – 'When I load the banana boat all night long . . .'

[6]

The party of ramblers seemed quite tame. They allowed me to approach them without huddling protectively and uttering their customary alarm call: 'Thisisarightofwayyouknow!' They were studying a field gate which carried a crudely lettered sign saying 'NEWLEY'. They asked me who this 'Mr Newley' was since they had come across his name on other gates scattered about the countryside. The answer is that he is not anybody. The sign is put there for the benefit of the Hunt. It indicates that the field beyond is a New Ley (newly-planted grass seeds) which will not be improved by being galloped over. This cannot but call to mind the classic remark on a TV farming programme that 'the secret of a good ley is a good firm bottom': no one is going to disagree with that.

[7]

I was up in the woods the other day, creeping quietly along the edge of a broad fire break. Tag, my German Wire-haired Pointer, always walks beside my knee when we are working. She suddenly stiffened and her nose started whiffing. There was a deer about. I froze, very carefully raised my binoculars and glassed the ride. Sure enough, amongst the thick heather at the wood edge about seventy yards away, I saw a twitching ear. We waited and after a minute or two a head appeared. It was a roe doe feeding quietly. Tag and I were standing right in the open but the wind was in our faces so our scent was blowing away behind us.

The doe raised her head and stared right at us. Now you might expect her to say to herself: 'Hot Damn! There's old Willy Poole with his bloody great bundook. I'm off!' but it does not work like that. All a deer sees is a duochrome shape in the ride. As long as that shape remains absolutely still, the deer does not necessarily regard it as a threat. We were immobile. After a long hard stare the doe dropped her head to graze and fed her way slowly across the open. A nose prodded my knee. The nose was saying: 'Bloody hell, Boss, get the deer shot – perfect position!' I scratched the old bitch's topknot with a finger. She does not understand about close seasons.

We watched the doe for about half an hour until she finally disappeared into the edge of the wood. Suddenly she came shooting out again, bouncing on stiff legs, stopped in the middle of the ride and stood there quivering and alert. Out of the wood behind her came a lovely big fox. He paid no attention to the outraged deer. I suppose that they must have met head on at the edge of the wood. The fox obviously had an interesting scent he was investigating. He had a good sniff round, cocked a leg and trotted back into the wood. The doe turned and bounded away into the trees on the other side of the ride. Tag and I walked on. Little scenes like this are all part of the fascination of the woods.

One day, earlier in the summer, I was creeping about below the crags at the top of the forest, in a straggle of stunted trees. I saw the little doe about fifty yards away. She was grazing quietly upwind of us and the dog and I were doing our famous impression of a sitka spruce. Then there was another movement in the heather and out came her kid. It could not have been more than a few days old, in full spotted camouflage and about the size of a small terrier. It gave a little skip and trotted up to its mother and immediately started to suckle. For about twenty minutes I stood stock still and watched entranced as the wee beast tucked into its breakfast. At last the doe decided that it was closing time and moved off with the, now very full, kid trotting behind her.

[8]

This has been a tremendous year for hares; I have seen a great number of leverets through the summer. Hares are interesting animals and steeped in folk lore. Country people always refer to a hare as 'she'. I suspect that it may have something to do with the once-held opinion that witches often changed into hares to go about their business.

Once upon a time there was a notorious witch in Bilsdale. In those days the Bilsdale Hunt (one of the oldest in England) hunted hare or fox. This day, hounds found a hare and had a good hunt with it and lost it. But then a report came of the hunted hare being seen crawling under the door of 'Awd Nellie's' shed. Having the reputation of being a witch, the general consensus was to leave well alone. But the huntsman was a robust character and no 'awd hag' was going to deprive his hounds of their quarry. He opened the shed door. No hare was found, but lying on the ground was 'Awd Nellie' breathing her last.

Hares are often referred to as 'Puss'. This is a corruption of its Latin name – *Lepus*. What I did not know until yesterday is that Puss was often kept as a household pet in days gone by – it seems that hares are easily domesticated. As they became superseded by cats, the name Puss got transferred. So what you thought was a cat is really a hare and if the hare turns into something else, please do not blame me.

[9]

This is a story for the opening of the Grouse Season. I am assured that it is true and if it is not, then it ought to be. The time is the early eighties. Now read on.

The old lady loved her grouse moor and after her husband died she continued to invite the same group of their old friends to come and celebrate the 'Glorious Twelfth'. Every year the little postcards with the unchanging message dropped through the same eight letter boxes and were looked forward to keenly by the old gentlemen concerned.

'Heard from Diana yet?' they would ask each other anxiously

as the summer progressed and just in case they had been over-looked this year.

'Going up to Diana's for the Twelfth again,' they would boast in the bar of Black's, once the card was safely on the mantelpiece: 'Oh really? Lucky you,' would be the respectful response.

The Twelfth dawned fine. McGudgeon the Head Keeper had reported that things were 'as weel as could be expectit' and things never got better than that with McGudgeon.

The old lady had an early breakfast with those guns who were staying in the house; Bertie Pole-Wiggley lived locally and would be joining them later. The breakfast conversation was much con-cerned with the miners' strike. The general consensus was that the miners were 'decent chaps'. The NUM leadership did not fare so well.

All of a sudden there was the sound of gravel being distressed by several hard-driven cars. There was much barking by massed dogs.

'Old Bertie's in a hurry. Eager for the fray, what?' said George Scures, wiping his moustache and going to the window. 'Good God! it's the rozzers! Hundreds of 'em! Forgotten your TV licence, Diana?' The old lady joined him at the window to be confronted by a line of police cars with flashing lights. What on earth was happening? She went to the front door and scooped up the Senior Terrier who had a short fuse and, although sadly short of teeth, was eager to give somebody a nasty gumming. As she opened the door a tinny voice boomed out: 'Armed Police! The house is surrounded! You cannot escape! Come out now with your hands up!'

The old lady found herself looking down the business end of various rifles and pistols, but she was having all her work cut out holding on to the Senior Terrier who was using some really rather regrettable language.

An old lady holding a struggling terrier is not a great threat object, but at that moment dear old Col. Pole-Wiggley came chugging up the drive in his battered Range-Rover with his ancient Labrador, Chunky, sitting beside him. The Colonel, with his game leg and purple face, had obvious criminal tendencies. He came in very handy for throwing on the ground and handcuffing. His comments on the situation in general and the constabulary in particular, delivered in Anglo Saxon, Hindustani and Arabic, were most illuminating. Chunky bit a policewoman.

From inside the house came the squashy sort of sound of elderly gentlemen being sat on by multiple policemen. Their collective language matched that of the Senior Terrier. The High Court Judge and the Lord Lieutenant were being particularly pithy. There was also the unmistakable sound of a coffee pot being broken over the upper slopes of a Detective Constable by the Lord Lieutenant's lady.

An Inspector got up from behind his car where he had been crouching, and approached the old lady. He had intended to address her as 'Sweetheart' but thought better of it at close range and made do with 'Madam' although he did wave a finger at her. The burthen of his speech was that he knew that the old lady was a dangerous terrorist and that her house was bristling with armed and dangerous men. However, thanks to the unceasing vigilance of the authorities, her dastardly plot had been discovered and would now be foiled. The Senior Terrier lunged at the Inspector who jumped back smartly but not quite quickly enough.

'Plot? What plot?'

'Ah ha!' said the Inspector (sucking his wounded finger) 'and how do you explain this then?' He flourished a copy of one of the old lady's invitation postcards and, because he rather liked it (as with Piglet and Kanga) and was flushed with adrenaline, he said, 'Ah ha!' once again. 'And what's more, *Madam*', continued the Inspector triumphantly, 'you couldn't even spell the little bugger's name right.'

The postcards had said exactly what they had said for the last thirty years: 'Come and help me shoot Scarghyll on August 12th.'

[10]

How things change in farming. When I sold butcher lambs, I took them to the Mart. There they had to be penned, graded and weighed, penned again, then they had to go through the auction ring, back to another pen, then onto the buyer's lorry and off to their final destination, which might be as far away as Dover. All of this consumed much of my time and put the lambs through a certain amount of stress. This did them no good and reflected on the payment that finally disappeared in to the black hole of my farm account. There must be a better way, I thought.

James Logan is one of the bright young men at County Auctions and one of the king pins in their Electronic Auction system. What is that? come with James and me and you will find out. We will start at the farm of the Graham family deep in profound Northumberland.

Willy and Grace Graham were hard at work in the pens when we arrived. They already had the lambs shed off from the ewes. The lambs were about 14 weeks old, fed on mother's milk and grass. They were 'Prime'; that is, ready for the butcher. The lambs were run through a 'race' (a narrow pen) so that James could handle and grade each lamb. Grading live sheep is a highly skilled job. By feeling the back and the tail of the sheep, the grader has to decide if they are right for slaughter and in the condition on the 'EUROP' scale that his buyers want. What is the scale? Take a piece of graph paper; write EUROP vertically – this is for conformation. Then on the top horizontal write 1 2 3L 3H 4L 4H 5 – this is the fat classification. Most good butchers' lambs would be in the U/R 2/3L range.

James worked fast with his marking crayon: back of head – too fat; unmarked – too plain; on the back – just right! Eighty-eight were drawn for sale: 'A good run of sheep'. Then it was back to the County Auctions office to watch the auction. At the office on a Friday morning the 'fieldmen' from all over the north telephone in the details of the lambs that they have drawn for their clients that morning. The details are then sent to the buyers. Anyone with a computer and a modem can play, always provided that they pay County Auctions for the privilege and that CA consider them to be genuine players. The buyers may be anywhere from Banchorie to Birmingham to Bedford. Each has a number.

As the appointed time approached, the computer consoles came alive: 'Starting in one minute' read the message on screen, then 'Sale about to commence'. Details of the first lot appeared on the screen: name of seller, number and type of sheep, collection point, weights, classification, method of feeding (e.g. grass/milk). The bidding started by the CA team typing in an offer price (e.g. 198 pence per kilo). On the screen the price drops a penny at a time until there is a bid. The buyer bids by pressing the enter button. The computer then ticks off 8 seconds. Any new bids have to be entered in that period, otherwise the computerised hammer falls (bleep) and the lot is sold.

Lot 55 W. A. Graham and Son (88 Suffolk X lambs – Av. weight 18.5 – Class R – Finish 3L/3H – Assessor J. Logan) were bleeped sold at 192p to buyer No. 5 (Canvin Int. Plc of Bedford). In all, 4,890 sheep were sold that afternoon whilst still grazing quietly in their fields. I do not think that the traditional Mart will ever fade, but the Electronic Auction does offer a convenience for both sheep and men. I wish that it had been around when I had lambs to sell.

And, finally . . .

I was reading a glossy magazine the other day. It is the sort of publication that concerns itself with the doings of what might be termed 'Café Society' – it does not have hunting reports. There was a picture of a wife of a pop star sitting on a horse with hairy legs (the woman that was – it said so in the piece). The caption said that the horse was kept in a 'heated open-air paddock'. I thought about this for a long time and then rang the magazine, in the name of Farmer's Diary, for clarification. The magazine thought about it for a long time and said that it was not glad that I had asked that question, but that it would get back to me. It never did. Does anybody know what a 'heated open-air paddock' is?

7. A BED FULL OF POLITICS

[1]

There is no doubt that many people in our urban island nation regard the indigenous country people as a collective pain in the base area – a backward and bloody people who interfere with the important things in life, like rambling and mountain biking – I mean, why can't these peasants get real? One of the ways to deal with troublesome Ab-originals is to get rid of them. Genocide is a method that has been used with some success in the past, but it does tend to be messy and might attract the attention of the

United Nations – whatever they are. No, there are less spectacular methods.

One of these methods is to jack up the cost of rural housing so that only people from the towns can afford to buy it – either as commuter, retirement or even holiday homes. There is a hamlet about a mile by the crow from where I am writing. In 1982 this hamlet consisted of two farms and a dozen or so houses – every house was occupied by an Ab-original. Now [1995] one of the farms is still working, the other has become a holiday cottage complex. All the houses are lived in now by Incomers. More towns people are seeking to live in the country and better cars and roads allow them to move further and further out. It is forty miles from here to the centre of Newcastle. Many people think nothing of commuting this distance on a daily basis. Ten years ago, this would have been almost unheard of. Mind you, none of these new commuters has had a seriously bad winter to cope with so far.

Because of this social movement, there are many rural young who have little prospect of being able to live, marry and bring up their children close to their roots. These young people will have little alternative but to go and live in the towns and become urban, whilst all the villages are taken over by towns people and become urban as well, in attitude, if not in fact. In this way, within fifty years there will not be any country persons and everyone will be as happy and as plastic as garden gnomes.

In its way this is as big a social revolution as that brought about by the Enclosures Acts of the eighteenth and nineteenth centuries. The enclosure of the Common Land forced the English peasantry into the towns to become factory fodder for the Industrial Revolution: 'The Law will punish man or woman/who steals a goose from off the common/but lets the greater felon loose/who steals the common from the goose.'

Affordable rural housing is one of the great problems of our time. The stock of council houses has diminished and has not been replaced. I know that Mrs Thatcher said that this would not happen, but even Mrs Thatcher could be wrong.

One idea has been to set up Housing Associations – 'independent, voluntary, non-profit-making organisations set up to provide social housing' – jolly good idea. The original idea included – 'funding from government . . . to cover a proportion of costs; the balance has to be raised from other sources.' You may care to think that this splendid idea has a certain dreamlike quality about it.

To build an affordable house there must be affordable land. In 1993 the Northumberland Land Bank was formed – 'to encourage landowners to offer suitable small plots of land at less than market value for the sole purpose of providing affordable housing for local people'. The idea has not provoked a flood of offers. The last figures that I have are – one firm offer and six 'possible'.

Then there are problems for landowners. The first is that they may offer some land at a cheap rate in return for planning permission on further land that can then be sold at the full market rate. The Planners do not like this – they call it 'Planning Gain' – it is not regarded as being politically correct. The second problem is that developers do not like 'Social Housing' next to their 'Executive Development' – urban yuppies do not like living next to the peasants. Peasants have cocks that crow and might have ferrets in the back garden. This knocks the value of 'neo-Georgian' hutches that the builders want to build.

The late President Ceaucescu had an answer to the rural housing problem. He just used to bulldoze villages and move the peasants into urban tower blocks where they could be 'controlled' – a very Politically Correct solution.

[2]

A friend of mine farms oysters on the lovely coast of Argyll. Now you and my friend and I might think that the untainted waters of the west of Scotland would be an ideal place for growing nice clean oysters. So it was, until a jolly little organism called '91/492/ EEC – Bivalve Mollusc Hygiene Order' came floating in on the tide: 492 wants all coastal waters classified A–E and you should be only looking to sell oysters from Class A (230 E.coli/100 g flesh; 300 faecal coliforms) waters. Should your water be in a lower classification, then your oysters have to jump through all sorts of veterinary hoops before you may present them to the public. Surely the oystermen of Argyll have no classification worries?

It seems, however, that preliminary tests are showing that only 50% of the Argyll sites are likely to be Class A. The Scottish Office rejected all independent assays. You may think that this shows an admirable zeal on the part of the EC for the health of its punters, but just consider this: all French sites and most of the Spanish have already been declared Class A. That may boggle your mind, but the Netherlands also gets straight As. So the filthy polluted waters of the Rhine delta that flow through Dutch oysters are of a higher purity than the clear pellucid waters of the Firth of Lorn or the Sound of Jura. There is a nasty whiff of political sewage about. We may now wait confidently for 'That Nice Mr Gummer' [as was Minister of Agriculture] to declare a stunning victory for British oyster farmers; then we shall know for certain that our producers have been sold out yet again.

I can quote an example at first-hand: political sewage.

Last week I flew to Portugal. It was a day of brilliant sun and clear sky. From the window I had a first-class view of a 'honey boat' discharging its cargo of effluent off Bournemouth. The slick seemed to be heading nicely inshore. The Bay of Biscay was unsullied blue until the coast of Spain. Here there was a grand scene of industrial sludge lakes, and a great brown river of filth flowing into the sea and spreading its foul brown stain along miles of Grade A coastline: just the stuff to add a bit of flavour to the oysters and quite safe, of course, because the EC has said so.

There is a simple answer to this: let the Buros of Brussels be lined up and stuffed with Continental oysters. If they survive, then we will believe them: but, if they first turn all the colours of the French tricolor and turn their toes up, we shall know that they got it wrong (again).

NOTE This was written in 1993. To the best of my knowledge and belief neither the pollution of European rivers nor the pollution of European politics has changed.

[3]

Various people have been asking me to share their hatred of wind farms. There is one planned for the top of Kielder Forest and local feeling, pro and con, is running high. One man assured me that the proposed wind farm would drive all the deer out of Kielder Forest and make it a wildlife desert. I begged leave to differ with the chap and to suggest that he was spouting emotional clap-trap. I have always liked windmills and I like the idea of wind farms, harnessing one of the resources that we have plenty of for free in this part of the world.

The only working wind farm that I have seen was in Cumberland. None of the locals to whom I spoke had any objection to the turbines. Far from 'desecrating the landscape' I thought that they added something to it with their great soaring towers and there was something rather comforting and fascinating in the great whirling blades harvesting the wind from off the Irish Sea. I would not mind having some on my farm.

In a few years' time, the wind towers will become an accepted part of the landscape and will play their part in saving 'finite fossil fuels'. The next furious row will come in the future when someone wants to pull down a wind tower; 'part of our heritage'; 'proposed official vandalism of a national monument'; 'hands off our wind towers'; etc. The sort of people making the fuss then will be exactly the same sort of people who are spitting in the wind now.

[4]

'Since time out of memory' is a useful phrase that seems to apply to many things in the countryside, but one should never underestimate the power of rural memory. For instance, I have an Irish friend who nurses a deep hatred for a certain noble English family. His reason for this strength of feeling is that in 15-something the incumbent English earl hanged sixteen members of my friend's family. I make no attempt to moralise in this matter, I just offer it as an example of rural memory. You may think that this is quite a stretch (no unfortunate pun intended) of memory, but I heard of one the other day that will take some beating.

Anyone who can remember the Year of Our Lord 993 will also remember that we were having trouble with the Danes at the time. The Danes of 993 were a bit different to the homogenised, pasteurised and thoroughly sanitised, blond bicyclists of today. You will remember that after the Romans took their ball and went home, the Angles and the Saxons came over and kicked seven kinds of manure out of the indigenous Brits, whose remnants disappeared into the Celtic mists of Wales and Cornwall. Then the Danes started sending out touring teams to give the Saxons a good seeing to. The Danes of the day were desperate keen on rapin', pillagin' and lootin' and in 993 were playing numerous matches all over what is now Gloucestershire.

We now cut to 1993. The Rural Dean was doing what rural deans do somewhere up in the Cotswolds. There were two small neighbouring villages that both had very large churches, relics of the days of the great wool prosperity. These churches were far removed from the needs of the small communities of 1993. The Rural Dean thought it would make sense if one church was kept to serve and save the souls of the two villages and the other one became a 'Redundant Church' within the meaning of the act. He took his idea to a parish meeting in Village A, where it was accepted as a sensible way of solving an increasing financial problem. The RD then went to a meeting in Village B. The idea was received badly. After the meeting, the RD, badly mauled, apologised to the Chairman of the Parish Council as he felt that he must have put his case very clumsily for it to get such a hostile reception. The Chairman placed a gnarled hand on his arm: 'Now, don't you worry, Dean. 'Tweren't nothing you did say but, you see, there's no way that we could fit in with they [Village A], they never come to help us when the Danes did come.'

[5]

I have before me the magazine of the National Trust, a very solid and sensible organisation, which I support. The membership of the NT is eclectic and the letters column can make for very interesting reading. Some of the writers seem to have strange ideas about the duties of the Trust. I liked the one from the woman who was not able to reach an ancient monument because of sheep droppings. She was doubly upset because of parents with 'small children finding it terribly difficult to watch their tiny feet and it was obviously creating stress'. Heavens to Murgatroyd! What a nation of wimps we are becoming! it was only a bit of sheep sh*t and the sheep were probably there before the ancient monument was a gleam in the collective eye of the Druidical District Council Planning Dept.

The lady writer must have little experience of small children if she thinks that they are going to be stressed by a bit of muck. When I was a Master of Hounds we used to have regular school visits to the Kennels. The high point was always the visit to the flesh house to watch a beast being skinned and cut up for the pot.

The children always loved this, although not a few of the escorting teachers would have to retire precipitately, especially when the time came to remove the plumbing ('Cor! look at that! what's them pink crinkly bits?') and demonstrate the bovine digestive system. Cutting up a beast is a somewhat messy business, but I never saw a child turn a hair; they used to have to be driven away. I remember one small boy who doubled back as the party was being herded off and asking if he could have a sheep's eye to take home to his mum, please? Now, he would not be worried about his tiny feet stabbling in a few sheep droppings.

Another letter demanded that the NT 'take immediate steps to encourage farmers to adopt organic and other alternative low-input sustainable agriculture (sic) practices'.

One of the prime reasons that farmers do not go organic is because it does not pay. One of the reasons that it does not pay is that people who faff on about organic produce will not actually buy it. Organic fruit and veg, for instance, comes warts, blemishes and all and does not always look as good as all that lovely-shiny-covered-in-chemical-sprays-and-fertiliser stuff. Also, the organic stuff costs more. When push comes to shove, your average Green likes the 'Idea', but not the 'Actuality'.

NOTE I am appalled by the National Trust's egregrious behaviour over stag hunting. I wrote in the *Daily Telegraph* that I would not trust the National Trust with a crooked sixpence.

[6]

I had an argument about hunting the other day with a fisherman. It has always surprised me that the same newspapers that condemn hunting on one hand, run angling competitions on the other. They, and my argumentative fisherman, might just have something of the Pharisee about them, as well as being rather Coarse.

I do not fish, but have no objection to anyone catching wild fish in a wild and natural state and then eating the result: this seems an entirely natural business and the fish is despatched cleanly once landed.

It does seem that some of the practices now apparently common amongst coarse fishermen are more than somewhat murky. The practice of buying salmon from fish farms and then stocking them in fresh water ponds can hardly be regarded as sporting, especially when you remember that salmon cannot feed in fresh water.

The practice of keeping fish in an overstocked pond and allowing them to be caught again and again should raise the odd ethical eyebrow. I know that someone is going to tell me that fish do not feel anything when they are hooked, but I would have to ask these people how they know that. I would also wonder whether stocked fish are not 'captive' within the meaning of the Wildlife and Countryside Act and what about the poor old farmed maggot wriggling on its hook? The EC has apparently exempted maggots from being 'captive animals', so that is all right then. There is now pressure to abolish the close season for coarse fish; fishery owners lose income in the close season. Many people might feel that this sort of fishing is no more sport than killing sheep in a slaughterhouse.

I was interested to be told by an official of the League Against Cruel Sports that many of his members are keen fishermen. No doubt they use humbug for ground bait: it all sounds pretty maggoty to me.

[7]

I charge the BBC with being politically incorrect. In particular, I charge it with Accentism. At one time when the Beeb Press Gang hauled young men and women off the streets and forced them into dinner jackets to make announcers of them, they also taught them to speak proper. The trainees were sent to an elocutionist equivalent of the old Guards Depot. There they polished their vowel (vial) sounds (sinds) until they gleamed, and huge men with waxed moustaches stood behind them and bellowed in their ears: 'AM I HURTING YOU, LAD??!!' 'No, Sergeant!' 'WELL, I SHOULD BE, I'M STANDING ON YOUR ****ING CONSONANTS!!' The graduates from this hell hole spoke with a strange strangulated accent that became known as 'BBC English'. The final repository of this strange sound was the old Radio 3. No doubt there are still dusty forgotten offices in Shepherd's Bush where bent old men tell each other what 'Lecky, Heppy Chepps' they are to be working for such a fine organisation (as who would not be). But now we are into the age of the Regional Announcer and Broadcaster. This is where my gripe really begins.

I am greatly in favour of regional accents and regard the moves by the educational establishment to abolish them as a form of verbal ethnic cleansing. Regional accents and patois should be preserved in all their glory and this is something that the BRITISH BC should be actively encouraging. They could do this by having *more* regional speakers on their air waves, thereby removing the stigma that some people feel attaches to dialect.

At the moment the only accents allowed on the Beeb appear to be 'South Eastern Polytechnic Nasal'; 'Ecky Thump General-Purpose Northern' and the token 'Scottish Neanderthal'. Can anyone produce an example of a genuine Cornish voice on air? The Spokespersons for 'Mabion Kernow' (Cornish Nationalists) all seem to speak with the accents of deepest Ruislip. There has been no Ol' Boy from Norfolk since the Singing Postman. Where are the splendid Anglo-Saxon HR sounds of rural Northumber-land (as in 'Hround the hrugged hrocks')? There might be those who would suggest that some accents might be too broad for general use and comprehension. However, the listener is expected to decipher the chain-saw-like sounds of token Ulstermen and to force his/her way through the tangled glottal stops of glamorous Glaswegians. Why not let us enjoy the buzzing burr of Wessex, the sing-song lilt of the Anglo-Welsh Borderland and eat linguistic 'tatty pot' from Cumberland? So let us hear it from the BBC for real regional accents. You never know, they might even take on a token Old Etonian; but that is really going into the realms of fantasy.

[8]

Now that it has become quite respectable for male and female persons to live together out of wedlock, there has been a certain amount of agonising amongst male members of the Chattering Classes about the correct method of describing 'the other half'. It is not PC to talk of 'lovers' or 'mistresses': could be some sexism lurking in there and we cannot be having that. It seems that 'partner' has become accepted as a suitably anodyne description and very boring it is too. I suppose that one has to convene a 'Partners' Meeting' every time that you want to have an 'in-depth discussion'. Is it necessary to have a third party present to take minutes?

It is typical of the Chattering Classes to think that they have suddenly invented a situation that has quietly maintained in remoter areas since Adam and Eve started it all. It is even more typical for the CCs to immediately start agonising about it. Up here in Northumberland, the problem of nomenclature was solved many years ago: a 'partner' is referred to as a 'bidey-in'.

A friend of mine went out hunting up in the hills. He was seen to be looking a little bemused and was asked how he was getting on. He replied that he would be getting on better if only the people spoke English. His problem came about because a lot of the words in current usage in the Borders are of an older and purer English than that which is now generally accepted. It is a fine thing that people should continue to speak as their forebears spoke. It is up to the incomer to learn where to find 'bield' (shelter) in bad weather and if he is told that hounds are 'gan like stoor', then he should understand that they are flying along like a cloud of dust. He should also understand that if he gets 'pallatic' in the pub and 'cowps', then he is likely to be 'hoyed oot' and quite right too.

[9]

A friend in London dearly loves a pork chop for her tea. She likes a nice fat juicy one with a kidney in it. 'A nice pork chop with a kidney, please, Mr Trotter,' she said to her friendly neighbourhood butcher. Mr Trotter took a sharp intake of breath, clicked his teeth, and shook his head until all his chins wobbled: 'Oh dear me, no, Madam,' says he. 'Can't do that no more, Madam, not if me life depended on it. Oh no, no, no.' 'Why not?' said my friend implacably. Poor Mr Trotter explained that he could sell Madam lots of lovely pork chops and lots of lovely kidneys, but not the one attached to the other. It was the EC, he was afraid; if it was left to him, Madam could have all the kidneyed chops that she wanted, but if the dreaded MAFF Food Police were to find out . . .

Soon after, Madam was visiting a friend in Bavaria, a convinced European. She attacked him about the iniquitous business of the Euro Pork Chop and its separate Euro Kidney. The Herr Graf rocked with Bavarian laughter and slapped his beefy thighs: 'You English,' he said, 'you are so stupid. You do not realise that EC rules and laws are just words and hot air [he actually used a more robust expression]. No one except the stupid English obeys them. Here, Liebchen, you may have all the pork chops with attached kidneys that you can eat.'

[10]

I am unhygienic. I expect that this 'coming out' will prompt a visit from the dreaded MAFF Thought Police whose lust for power has prompted them to introduce a whole load of useless and sometimes downright dangerous regulations. Do you remember the business over ripping out all wooden shelving and the ritual burning of wooden chopping blocks? It has now been proved that wood is healthier than plastic after all.

Anyway, back to my personal problem. In fact, it is a problem with most country people; we are simply not Hygienically Correct. Many is the time I have spent the morning 'cowing' sheep. This operation entails removing the rags of soiled wool from the nether end of a sheep with a pair of hand shears; this is done in the interests of animal welfare and, yes, hygiene. After a morning at this interesting and absorbing work, I would sit down and get out my bait bag, having first wiped my hands carefully on my trousers. There is no doubt that the basic essence of sheep does impart a certain, subtle *je ne sais quoi* to the sarnie and if the corner you have been holding does look a little blacker than you fancy, the collies certainly will have no qualms about it.

There is a good old rural saying: 'You'll eat a peck of dirt before you die', suggesting that honest dirt never hurt anyone. In all my bucolic life I can only remember one rustic succumbing to food poisoning and that was caused by supermarket prawns which must go to show something or other. Mind you, there are limits even to my disdain for hygiene. I once went to the local knacker yard, where Bert was up to his elbows in removing the internal plumbing from several rather distantly deceased sheep. Being a cheerful soul, Bert always liked to stop for a chat and thought that he might as well eat his 'crib' (elevenses) while he was at it. He gave his reeking hands a perfunctory wipe on his boiler suit, got down his tin box and took out a sandwich. He was kind enough to offer it to me. I gracefully declined and hastily lit my pipe.

Now there is another thing and a parenthesis. I am sure that it is only a matter of time before the Fragrant Mrs Bottomley [then Minister of Health] rules that pipe smokers will need the equivalent of a Fire Arms Certificate before they can pursue their simple pleasure. I suppose that I shall have to go back to smoking mine up the chimney, like I used to do at Eton.

Back to hygiene: I remember many years ago going with my mother to visit a lady who had come straight from the cowshed to the making of pastry which did look a funny grey colour. My mother very bravely suggested that it might have been better had she washed her hands first:

'Oh, get home do!' came the response. ' 'Twill all come off in the flour,' and it did: *bon appetit.*

8. POOLE'S PEREGRINATIONS

[1]

To the US of A for the greater glory of the *Daily Telegraph*. A battered pick-up truck with a dog in the back; a man in a black Stetson who was chewing tobacco: instinct told me that they had got to be there to meet me and I was right.

The place was San Antonio (Texas) airport, the dog was Sandy and the weather-beaten man was Mike Wren, my guide, companion and mentor in the days to come.

Mike Wren is a fascinating man: rancher, ex-rodeo rider and

professional hunter. He kindly invited me to his home near Kerr-ville to meet his charming wife Marilyn and the three boys of whom he is justly proud. Mike was a rodeo man of note, specialising in 'Bull-Dogging' (diving from a galloping horse onto a galloping steer and wrestling it to the ground) and Steer Roping. It is not surprising that he is lame. The two elder boys both have Rodeo Scholarships at Sul Ross University. The youngest boy is still at school and is already World Junior Team Roping Champion.

I was invited to watch them practise 'Dally Roping', which is their especial skill and works thus: a steer is released from a chute. The steers are wily, wiry Mexican Corientes, lean, mean cattle: 'Ain't good for nothin' but ropin'.' The two riders on their clever Quarter (c. $10,000) horses go from a standing start to max revs. There is the Head Roper and the Heel Roper. The Head Roper drops his noose around the steer's horns. The Heel Roper, on the other side of the steer, ropes (would you believe) its heels. The well-trained horses then spin to a stop. The ropes are turned round the saddle horns ('Most ropers got fingers missin''). The two ropers should then be facing each other, their ropes taut, and the steer still standing, but immobilised, between them. The horses will move of their own accord to keep the ropes tight. Dead easy! but just remember that it is all done at a gallop and against the clock. It should take about eight seconds. Like all rodeo displays, this has a practical application. It is the best method of catching scrub-wild cattle for operations such as branding, or veterinary treatment. The skill of these young men was truly impressive. The rodeo world expects them to go far and I do not doubt that they will.

The cattle business is not too brilliant in the US of A. 'But what,' I hear you cry, 'about farming?' It seems that the Agri-Business with the economy of scale is doing 'pretty good'. It is the small family farms that are catching it in the neck. When I travelled in Georgia and Alabama, there were constant reminders of failure: tumble-down board houses and acres of land reverting to scrub and rough grazing. In this part, the money spinners are the three

'Ps' – Pecans, Peanuts and Pines (for timber). I met a lady whose family was jogging along with 150 thousand acres of pines: then they struck oil on the property. I guess that they are now just managing to get by.

Wealth is not always conspicuous in the USA. I sat in company with a man whom I had always known to be a cattle man. In the conversation it transpired that he also had an interest in a TV station. He had recently had a substantial offer for this which he had refused. When I quizzed him, he replied, 'Well, I look at it this way, $30 million aren't going to make no difference to my life style.'

You often hear people sneering about American food. I do not know where they have eaten, but it was certainly not anywhere that I have been. I have always eaten well, from Marilyn Wren's memorable chicken fried steak to Brunswick stew in Alabama (watch out for the 'squill' – squirrel – heads) through succulent fried catfish in Georgia, by way of wonderful Bar-B-Q beef and venison in Texas with diversions into Tex-Mex and some memorable Jalapenos (small green peppers, stuffed with cheese and deep fried in batter, which made me the fastest man in the West) to a truly Lucullian Brunch in California. Only the English could manage to eat badly in America.

When in America, do as the locals do. Here are some useful tips for travellers that I will offer: for instance, should you visit the Lone Wolf Lounge deep in the heart of the Texas hill country (a place with sawdust on the floor and where you stare straight ahead when sitting at the bar) do not take your hat off, do not ask for wine and do not get mistaken for a Yankee. As Mike, my guide and mentor, said: 'Ain't it a bummer when y'all got to fight yoh way out?' By the way, the same advice applies for a visit to Krones Store and Bar somewhere deep in the swamp land of Alabama, especially the Yankee bit. Do remember that the South never fought a Civil War; it was 'The War of Northern Aggression' and y'all better mind that, less'n y'all want yoh ass busted but good. Yessuh!

[2]

I had not been in Texas before and I was there to hunt 'Exotics' – thereby hangs an explanation.

Back in the 'twenties and 'thirties ranchers in Texas started introducing wild animals from foreign climes to their land, animals such as sable antelope from the Middle East, impala and Grants gazelle from Africa, blackbuck and axis deer from India, moufflon sheep from Sardinia and many others. All come under the heading of 'Exotics'. Texan ranchers are hard-headed people. They did not bring in all these animals and turn them loose on their ranches for purely aesthetic or environmental reasons. They brought them in so that people with money would pay to come and hunt the Exotics and go away with a trophy and rather less money than they arrived with. Before the hysteria sets in, it is as well to consider the practical outcome of all this. The animals have thrived and multiplied in the scrubby hills of Texas, to the extent that there are now thought to be more blackbuck and axis deer in Texas than there are in India. So the hard-headed Texans have achieved an environmental dimension to their business venture: they could indeed be said to be 'doing well by doing good'.

The Flying A Ranch is near Bandera ('The Cowboy Capital of the World'). This is the Texas 'hill country' – miles of rolling volcanic hills covered in scrubby live oaks, cactus, rocks and coarse grass. This used to be high-plain country where the buffalo roamed and where the Comanche and Kiowa did their thing. One of these things was to set fire to the plains on a regular basis to improve the grazing. Now the Comanche and Kiowa are no more so the plains are scrub. This land will support cattle at c. 1 cow to 23 acres, but it certainly supports a whole lot of Exotics. The Flying A (c.50,000 acres) is owned by Mr Albert Alkek, who is 'in oil'. He no longer lives in the beautiful 130-year-old ranch house which is now available for hunting guests. The hunting (hunting in the USA usually means shooting) rights are leased by the Texas Safari Co. which is British: hooray! Mike Wren is the man on the spot. He is Texican bred and buttered from a ranching family. He has punched cows, ranched, been on the rodeo circuit and for over twenty years he has been a professional hunter. He is an acknowledged expert on Exotics. He is also an expert on hats and I had to get a hat – for the sunstroke, you see. I had left England in the grip of snow, floods and ice. In Texas the sky was a brilliant blue and the temperatures ranged from freezing nights to the high 70°sF in the day. It felt good and so did the hat, a magnificent black 5x beaver 'Lane Frost' (a famous, but deceased, bull rider: it is quite easy to become a deceased bull rider) 10-galloner from Hackett the Hat. It took time. Buying a hat in Texas is a serious business. The hat has to reflect your size, shape and personality and has to be steamed, twisted and dented accordingly. So how did I look? 'Like 100,000 acres, I guess,' said Hackett.

Business concluded and a light brunch of hot cakes, syrup and bacon eaten, we set off for a tour of the Hondo West section of the ranch. The ranch is well served with tracks and the animals take little notice of vehicles, until they stop. Step out of the truck and they are gone like the wild animals they are. Over the hill behind the Hondo West ranch house we drove through a great park-like expanse, where red deer, sika deer and the lovely black-buck with their spiral horns were all feeding along with a herd of at least a hundred axis deer. It was a truly amazing sight to be savoured. As comic relief, we watched an armadillo whiffling about for its tea; what jolly little things they are.

As we drove, we sighted groups of animals all the time, feeding or lying in the shade. Then we saw the three big moufflon rams, magnificent brown and black animals with great curling horns, about 300 yards away.

'OK, pardner,' said Mike, 'let's do it,' and he took the rifle from the rack. For an hour we crept, crawled and slipped from tree to tree, trying to get within the range of the three old gentlemen until they eventually disappeared into the thorn scrub on the mountain and the evening shadows.

'Well,' said Mike, pushing his hat back, 'them big ol' boys didn't live to get that big by being dumb. We better go get ourselves a beer.' Amen to that: I was, as they say in Texas, 'Drier'n a popcorn's f--t.' That night we ate Mexican. 'If'n it don't make you sick, it's good.' It did not make me sick and it was good. It also made me the fastest Limey in Texas. Mexican food is to be highly recommended for anyone feeling costive.

The Texas dawn was wonderful; a rind of frost, a brilliant blue sky and a huge sun peeping over the horizon, promising later heat.

We drove out into Hondo West, past herds of axis, blackbuck and sika. Then we debussed and set off on foot across the scrubby, cactus- and mesquite-larded plain. The morning air was crystal sharp on the lungs.

We stopped frequently to glass the ground in front of us which was now rising towards a large rocky hill. There was a flicker of movement in the live oaks, beyond a clearing. We sank down behind a clump of mesquites and got the binoculars up. In the shadow of the trees was a group of Corsican sheep, including a magnificently horned ram. When we talk of sheep, you must forget the placid woolly things you see grazing in English fields. These are wild mountain sheep; sharp as fitch ferrets and as wild as weasels. Mike tapped my shoulder and we crept forward. The sheep were on the move: 'The thing with sheep is they keep moving and y'all got to just follow on and hope that they make a mistake.' So we crept as quietly as we could on the loose, slithery stones that constituted the hillside. For some forty minutes we saw no more. Then as we crept up to a clump of cedar, there was a tiny movement in the scrub above us. We froze. And there he was, the Big Ram, standing on a rocky spur about 100 yards away. Just in front of us was a stunted bush and a rock for an ideal rest: unsling the rifle – inch forward in a leopard crawl – take the rest – bring the cross hairs on the scope to a point just behind the shoulder, a good, clear, honest shot – breathe out gently – squeeze the trigger and . . . S★★T!! A clean miss! I could try the excuse that it was a strange rifle, but I do not think that I will bother and, anyway, Mike, kind man that he is, did it for me. There was only one thing to do – stalk on.

There was real warmth in the sun and the 'cold Bud' (weiser) was welcome as we bumped and ground our way to a new area on Section 2. We saw the moufflon almost at once – three good old rams with some young rams and perhaps twenty ewes. They also saw us and waited not upon the order of their going. We set off on foot. The sheep were heading into the mountain with its slopes of sliding stone and thick thorn scrub. The sun was high now with the temperature in the high 70°sF, but there was a cooling breeze. I am not sure how long we crept, crawled and climbed about those rocky slopes and, by the way, if you do slip and fall, do not do it onto a patch of cacti. Cacti make a lasting impression. In our stalk we got occasional glimpses of the sheep, usually just disappearing. At last we reached the top of the mountain and crawled forward to where there was a good view down the scrubby slope beyond. They were filing quietly across the open about 150 yards away and there, bringing up the rear, was one of the old rams. Mike touched my shoulder. Once more I got into position – cross hairs on – breathe deeply – exhale – squeeeeeze the trigger – the old gentleman dropped like a stone. Mike punched my shoulder and we shook hands: 'Hot damn, Boy! y'all did good!' It certainly felt that way.

On my last morning, Mike handed me the rifle and told me to go out on my own: 'Shoot what you like.' I walked up the hill behind the ranch house. It was another morning of warm sun and cool breeze. The air in Texas is something else; believe it. Walking quietly but normally, I reached the top of the hill and there were four Catalina billies (goats) with their twisted horns. I was working across the wind. They had not seen me, but were suspicious. There was one magnificent billy, but there was also a younger billy with a broken horn and lame on his near fore. I trailed them for about an hour until I came up behind a large live oak and there they were, standing in a bunch across a small valley; estimated range 70 yards. I sat and watched them for about ten minutes. I might have got broken horn, but the big billy was close beside and beyond him: not a permissible shot. 'Anyway,' I thought, 'b****r it.' So I sat in the sun with my back against the tree and lit my pipe and watched the goats move quietly away. I felt mightily content. This was more than could be said for the raven who circled me all the way back to the ranch, croaking dismally. He obviously thought that, as a hunter, I was not even a good journalist.

The Flying A Ranch was a great experience and so is Texas. As we shook hands at the airport, Mike said: 'Y'all come back soon, y'hear.' I shall be back; y'all better believe it.

[3]

A Holy Nun nicked my luggage at Knock airport. To be fair, Sister Brigid's case did look a bit like mine and she was in a hurry to get to the nunnery. We got it all sorted out in the end, although what the good sister thought when she opened her case and found a Gent's Natty Whistle, a shaving kit and a pair of underpants that would make a fair bell tent, is not on record.

'Why are you going to Co. Mayo?' they asked. The perfectly truthful reply – that I was going there to eat oysters – seemed to bring out the green-eyed monster in most people. 'Why you?' they snarled. I told them to address their queries to my hosts – *Bord Lascaigh Mhara* (Irish Sea Fisheries Board for those who do not speak Erse).

Mayo seems to consist mostly of bits of bog loosely stitched together with barbed wire. It has a certain wet and windswept charm. I would not like to try and make an agricultural living there. And yet, said one of the party, there were a lot of smart-looking, newish agricultural bungalows about. As British tax-paying contributors to the EU we all owned several breeze blocks in each house.

Westport is a charming old coastal town and if you go there I recommend the Olde Railway Hotel without any hesitation – it is everything that a hotel ought to be. Not that there was much time to enjoy its comforts because it was on with the wellies and out into Clew Bay ('The Bay of the Thousand Islands') on Matt Mulloy's mussel dredger – almost everybody in Mayo seems to be called Mulloy.

Mussels are not exciting creatures – you dangle a net in the water and mussels grow on them and when you have seen one line of mussels . . . They became much more exciting when hot, steaming, fat and delicious from Matt's galley. There are certain moments that stick in the memory – eating fresh mussels on a dredger in the soft rainswept twilight in Clew Bay is one of them.

'Bio Salmon Farming' is the buzz phrase. Farmed salmon tend to be somewhat flabby and lack the flavour of the wild fish. The Irish are trying to produce a better quality of farmed salmon by putting their cages further out to sea where the currents sweep through them and the Atlantic gales buffet them with 16-metre waves. This makes the salmon more muscular and cuts down problems of parasites and infection. These 'High Seas' salmon farms, along with the various processing and smoking plants, are dotted along the coast of Co. Mayo and Co. Connemara. This is the '*Gaeltacht*' where Erse is still the first language – speak Irish and your business gets an extra dollop of EU taxpayers' money.

The west coast is jagged with bays and inlets. To go from a salmon farm one side of the bay to a fish processing plant on the other might mean forty miles on twisting roads – but in a helicopter it takes five minutes. A helicopter is a grand way to travel – unless you put a quart of persons into a pint-pot of a chopper. It is also a grand way of looking down at fish cages heaving up and down in the Atlantic swell. As the pilot banks enthusiastically yet again, the plunging horizon disappears yet again and the only thing to do is to hold out one's tweed cap to the lady journalist sitting opposite – just in case. The situation was not eased by circling (after the fifth circuit, people start waving to you) in search of a processing plant that ought to have been there, but which had been moved in the night (leprechauns?) or so the pilot swore – still you can always land and ask the way.

Fishing, farming and Bed & Breakfast for students of Gaelic are the main industries on this rugged storm-swept coastline. Connemara is mostly rock and bog. Tiny crofts cling to the strip of hard-won grazing land on the edge of the sea. Looking down from the air at the mass of small fields with their higgledy stone walls, one suspects that EU grants might be the main crop.

Apart from salmon, the coast produces oysters, mussels, clams, winkles and wonderful crabs and lobsters. The Irish do not eat much fish – almost everything goes for export. It is passing strange, I mused to myself as I put away the first dozen oysters of the day (10.30 am) that we in the UK eat only 600 tons of oysters per annum. France (with much the same population) stuffs away *145 thousand tons*. Ah well, close my eyes and eat for England – another dozen? well, why not?

[4]

They decided that I was definitely an honorary 'Coon Ass'. Before you all say that you had worked that out yonks ago, you had better know what one is and also know that I consider it a great honour. I had been visiting Avery Island in Louisiana. Avery Island is the home of Tabasco Sauce, which is owned by the McIlhainy and Avery families who also own the island (since 1827), and only members of the two families may have permanent residence there.

The island is the peak of a solid mountain of salt which sticks out of the Bayou – the swamp lands of the Mississippi delta. This day it was decreed that we go for a 'Crawfish Boil' at the Trappers' Hut. It was a day of brilliant sun and cool breeze, which made the locals huddle into winter clothing – in Northumberland it would have been a hot summer's day.

We set off into the Bayou on the Tabasco launch and continuous Bloody Marys – it is a matter of regret that the magnificent Tabasco Bloody Mary Mix is not available in the UK, for reasons that I still do not understand. The Bayou is fascinating – a series of snaking waterways that run through twisted swampy woodland, interspersed with great stretches of reedy savannah. The Trappers' Hut was a little wooden hut on stilts up a secret creek in the savannah which can only be reached by boat. The Bayou is sprinkled with these huts, for this is Cajun Country, populated by French-speaking people who originally lived in Nova Scotia which they called 'Acadia' (Arcadia) until the wicked Brits drove them out. The Cajuns (Acadian gone a bit slurred) were originally farmer/hunter/gatherers who lived off the land and got a little cash by trapping and selling pelts. Thus they were 'simple people who live close to the land' – for which the old Carib Indian word is 'Kunaso'.

The crawfish were already on the boil when we arrived, supervised by Lon Prioux and three other Coon Asses. Before luncheon, Lon took us for a ride in his 'airboat'. This is a flat-bottomed boat driven by an aeroplane propeller which, in turn, is driven by a truck engine. With one of these you skim through shallow water and over mud flats. We saw alligators (18 feet is the record), snowy egrets and green-backed herons. The Bayou has no pollution and is a great haven for wildlife.

The crawfish ('mud bugs', 'craw daddies') are mostly farmed now. They grow them in the rice fields after the harvest. The boiled article was just tipped out in great scarlet heaps on the wooden tables on the porch, along with sweetcorn and *andouille* (a spicy sausage guaranteed to clear out your sinuses). Oh My Dears! how we guzzled and grunted and guzzled some more, to an average consumption of c. 5.2 lbs per person. Then it was the rocking chair on the porch, the pipe in one hand, a can of beer in the other and time for swapping yarns. It was when the Cajuns twigged that I was an even bigger liar than they were that they awarded me the accolade of honorary Coon Ass-ship. I am very honoured. I felt very at home with the Cajuns, but this only goes to bear out my theory that country people are pretty much the same the world over.

I have just returned from my trip to Louisiana and when you read this I shall be packing my red-spotted hanky to go to Austria. In these days of almost universal travel it is refreshing to find people who have no wish to gad about the world. I am reminded of a friend of mine who was talking to a crofter on Jura. The friend asked the old man if he had ever been to the mainland. The crofter pondered on this and then said, 'No, but I have travelled extensively on Jura.'

[5]

To Austria – to do some research for my first novel, *The Hounds of Heaven.*

'You'll love Vienna,' they said, 'and of course you will go to Salzburg.' I hated Vienna. Mind you, I only saw the ring road and the airport and I did not go within spitting distance of Salzburg. My researches took me to the deeply rural area between the Danube and the Alps and to the high plateau country towards the Czech border. This area sees few tourists and vice versa. It is extremely beautiful country of steep hills and deep wooded valleys – it reminded me a bit of North Devon writ large.

This is an area of peasant farms – the average farm size is c.30 acres – and the thing that pleased me was how prosperous it all looks. The farmhouses and steadings are substantial and beautifully kept and seem quite out of proportion to the farming operations. Austria is a country of peasant farmers and the politicians have been very mindful of this fact – subsidies have been extremely generous. The farmers are not happy about the EU (Austria joined at the beginning of 1995) as they fear cuts in their subsidies. However, I am sure that Austrian politicians will find a way to pacify them. Like every other EU country except Britain, Austria knows that EU laws are for passing, not for obeying, and that the main purpose of the EU is to relieve British and West German taxpayers of large sums of money – *Gruss Gott*.

'*Gruss Gott*' is what you say when you walk into a pub or shop in Austria. Do not walk into too many shops unless you are rich – Austria is very expensive. I walked into a number of pubs – local colour, you understand – and very jolly they were, too. I wear one of those green felt Austrian hats for stalking and I took it with me. Almost every peasant wears a similar hat and a large moustache, so my camouflage was good – to the extent that there was great surprise to find that I was an Englander. The English are rare birds in those parts and it was generally decided that I must be a Lord, a very pardonable mistake.

It was in one of the pubs that I met Obstler. Obstler is a pear and apple schnapps. I had one pressed on me as a digestive after a large luncheon of pig meat – in rural Austria it tends to be the pig, the whole pig and nothing but the pig. When I left this particular pub, the landlord presented me with half a side of bacon – bacon, home reared, home killed and home cured: this would no longer be allowed in Britain, but Heaven help the EU official who tries to come between the Austrian peasant and his pigs.

But back to Obstler, which made a profound impression on me. I tossed the first one back with the approved cry of '*Prosit*'. Large hands patted me on the back as I choked and spluttered – it was an oral stun grenade, home-made and double the strength of whisky. When I recovered, it seemed meet and right to have another. The world was looking good and the talk was of farming and stalking – the peasants are keen *Jagers*. Then came a mouth-watering chocolate cake (diet? what diet?) with 'Jesus, Mary and Joseph' – 'sweet, sharp and hot': take a large glass, put in Obstler, sugar and then fill up with black tea – delicious. I do not know what Jesus, Mary and Joseph would do for you, but they made me sing.

[6]

Not long ago, I attended Mass at a village church in central France. As I was waiting, I looked around the church. On the north wall was a large and flamboyant plaque to 'The Glorious Dead' of the 1914–18 war. There were forty names on the plaque. This was a scattered rural parish and a village of, perhaps, seventy houses. It is hard and painful to try to imagine the shattering effect that so many deaths must have had on a small peasant community. It is little wonder that the French did not want to see a repeat of that slaughter in 1940.

On the south wall of the church was a small discreet plaque that was put up after the Hitler war. It recorded no deaths, but thanked God for 'the return of our prisoners of war and of Elisabeth de *******, deportée'.

Those two plaques gave me some inkling into the agony of France in the course of this century and as to why the only war that gets discussed at the French dinner table is the Hundred Years War.

There are two sides to every coin. In contrast to the French war memorial mentioned above, I looked at an Austrian memorial in a very similar village and counted over a hundred names of men killed or missing. Against most names was the word '*Rusland*'. Most of the men from this area went to the Eastern Front. Most went to Stalingrad. Most did not come back. What a bloody waste.

[7]

I love Port, but I do not pretend to be an expert in this most expert of subjects. 'Always go to the top,' is a good *modus operandi* and so an invitation from Alistair Robertson (Chairman of Taylor,

Fladgate and Yeatman) to visit Oporto was something to be savoured and run round the taste buds and certainly not to be spat out.

Taylor's have been in the Port trade since 1692, so we have been drinking Portuguese wine for some 300 years. The original table wines did not respond well to travel. Brandy was added to the wine, which solved the problem and also produced the unique, succulent and luxurious wine that all right-thinking people love and respect.

So it was the BA Saturday flight to Oporto (more properly Porto) on a day of cloudless sky and 90-degree heat, then a short drive to Gaia where the Port Houses all cluster above the river.

Portugal is a place of delight: a place to lie in a hammock in the shade of a custard apple tree, with blue sky above and a pleasant breeze to soothe the fevered brow of the traveller. On one side, the bougainvillaea might riot along the huge uncut stone blocks of an old monastery wall. On the other side, there might be a fig tree close at hand, in case you felt in need of a snack. Should you have packed that tiresome Protestant Work Ethic, then a plunge into the sun-warmed pool would drown the beggar. Journalism can be hell.

In the evening I explored Porto and especially those parts pertaining to the Port trade. The Factory House is the equivalent of a Livery Hall for the Port Houses. This is a splendid building with an amazing granite staircase and wonderful vaulted ceilings. In the library there are ancient traders' maps. An 1835 map of Africa is mostly blank, but shows Zimbabwe inhabited by the 'Moombos – said to be shepherds, but Cannibals' and if you have ever wondered why Canada? it would seem to derive from the two Portuguese words: Ca Nada – Nothing Here. There are two dining-rooms with identical tables: the assembled company dines in one room and takes Port in the other.

A walk down to the old quay was worthwhile. Across the river were all the Port Houses: Calem, Sandeman, Croft, Offley, Taylor's, Dow . . . the very names make one salivate. The real salivation started on entering Taylor's Lodge: the amazing, vinous

smell of 8,000 pipes of Port, great lines of them crouching huge
and gravid in the dim light. Why pipe? The Port trade uses ancient
measures: a Pipe (c.100 gallons) was the most a two-ox-power
cart could carry; an Almude (25 litres) the most that a woman
could carry on her head and a Canada (2 litres) the most a man
should drink in one day and Amen to that.

Back to dinner through the dusk and the blaring streets with
the inevitable snap, crackle and pop of fireworks: the Portuguese
love noise.

A glass (or two) of Port was taken after dinner.

Sunday was a big day. It was the day of the annual *Barco Rabelo*
race. The *barcos rabelos* were the original wine barges. They used
to go up the Douro by wind and muscle power, taking about three
days to the Upper Douro. They would collect the pipes from the
quintas (vineyards) and run back down with the current, riding
the white-water rapids in considerable peril. In the 60s, the
Government dammed the river and killed the barge trade. The
barges were left to rot. Ten years ago the Port Houses decided to
each have a barge and hold an annual race, from the harbour bar
to the main quay in Oporto. Each House now has one of these
strange, Viking-shaped, flat-bottomed barges. The barges are
driven by a huge square sail to take advantage of the prevailing
westerly wind that blows up the Douro. Each sail carries the
insignia of the House. The boats are crewed by enthusiasts from
the Houses, but the helmsman, on whom so much depends, is
usually a local fisherman who understands the intricacies of the
Douro. The barges are steered by a huge stern oar.

Down at the quay the Confraria de Vinho do Porto was
assembled in full fig of robes, Rembrandtesque hats and *tastevins*
hung around necks. With their acolytes and followers, the Brethren
all piled onto a waiting motor boat. In case this suggests urgency,
do not be deceived. 'This may take some time,' applies to most
things in Portugal. *Horas Inglesas* (English hours) is an expression
used to indicate punctuality in Porto.

The excursion was diesel powered but we were driven by a

never-failing supply of chilled white Port as we slipped downstream to the harbour bar where the boats were already lined up. Time for another glass of Port.

The klaxon sounded, some of the inevitable fireworks were let off and the brightly coloured square sails were frantically raised. Did Sandeman's jump the klaxon? that is not for me to say, but they quickly went into a commanding lead. There seemed to be a bit of bumping and boring between Cockburn and Graham who then seemed to be attempting to board Dow. Some nifty work with boat hooks by Dow's hardy men repelled their advances. Another glass? well, thank you very much; delicious.

Warre was going well in the middle of the field. Croft, Cockburn and Dow had gone into a huddle and appeared to be heading for the rails. Help myself? thank you.

There was little wind, but Sandeman's coxswain obviously knew of a cunning current and was increasing the lead. Approaching the big road bridge, Sandeman came right across the river to the Porto side. The wind was very fluky in the gorge and the field began to close on the leaders, with Offley badly tailed off. Thank you, I do not mind if I do.

I am sorry to report that the race ended somewhat inconclusively and in confusion. This was no doubt due to the lack of wind and the fact that the hour of luncheon was approaching, something of great importance in Portugal.

Vargellas is Taylor's *quinta* on the Upper Douro. From the lush coastal plain, the road climbed into the harsh rock-strewn hinterland, with its great granite tors and wandering flocks of horned sheep attended by wild-looking shepherds. Then came the first amazing sight of the Douro valley and the corkscrew descent, through the precipitous vines, to the jewel that is Vargellas, with the long white house on the hillside above the river. Vargellas consists of the house, the farm and the railway station.

It was a memorable Sunday evening with a 20-year-old Tawny Port before dinner. There was a tiny Japanese lady journalist who had to be introduced to the intricacies of after-dinner Port

(Taylor's '70) drinking, all of which she noted in minute detail in a minute book. I longed to ask her how she managed to spend a month travelling around Europe with nothing but a T-shirt and shorts, a large handbag and a camera case; an example to us all in frugal efficiency.

The evening was made more memorable by an electric storm and a decanter of Quinta de Vargellas '65, which I consider to be one of the most delicious, luscious Ports that I have ever tasted. Then the lights went out. We sat on the terrace (with yet another decanter of Vargellas '65) entranced by the *son et lumière* of the storm over the mountains.

Monday came fresh and clear, billowing with the scent of flowers and loud with bird song. I was only just in time. That day saw the end of the picking. The weather had been good and the vintage cool and dry. It was finishing a week ahead of normal.

Alistair Robertson and his wife, Gillyanne, hold court at Vargellas during the vintage and host a continuous stream of thirsty pilgrims and hacks. The main house sits on the hill above the farm and the winery. As we drank white Port on the terrace, a strange rhythmic thumping noise floated up the hill – the 'Cut' had started.

Taylor's are one of the very few who still rely on 'Pedal Maceration' – the 'Pisa' – oh all right, 'treading', then. Each day's pick of grapes is put into a huge granite tank (5,000 litres) – a *lagar* – to about knee depth. The pickers, male and female, form into two ranks that stretch the width of the *lagar*. They put their arms round each other and with set faces (this is serious stuff) they march up and down the tank in time to a monotonous chant from a sort of Regimental Sergeant Major – this is the Cut. The words of the chant translate as 'Liberty, Ah Liberty / only to a few you're known / if only I had liberty / just to call my feet my own'.

We went back to dinner. We dined well. After dinner we drank Port – delicious Port (Vargellas '67 and 20-year-old Tawny) – rather a lot of delicious Port – then we went dancing. As we walked down the cobbled track in the starlight, the sound of music floated up from the winery – they were dancing in the grapes. This is the 'Mix', the next stage of pedal maceration.

After the serious business of the Cut, the treaders loosen up a bit. In comes a man with an accordion or, in this case, an electronic keyboard and they dance. 'Absolutely bacchanalian, my dear,' said a very distinguished wine writer. I have to tell you that if you take distinguished writers and fill them with Port and stick them in a *lagar*, they dance like stoats. 'Hey, man, let's macerate!' cried a well-known lady Food and Drink Editor, leaping into the gunge – it is rather like what I imagine dancing in knee-deep Scotch Broth must be like. It is very messy – 'The workers' knees are deepest red.'

I must say that Portuguese ladies are extremely comely when young but tend to ripen quickly – my partner was about the same size as me, but her moustache was bigger. The Portuguese make no concessions to modern dance forms – every kind of tune is treated as a two-step. However, they have taken to the Conga in a big way. It all sounds (and is) great fun, but it is a serious matter with a great deal of money at stake.

The Pisa is a traditional method that has been followed for hundreds of years. It is labour intensive and labour costs are rising. There are other vinification methods – 'Autofermentation', 'Rotovats', the 'Mechanical Foot' (it went lame), the 'Movie Mosto' and 'Static Fermenters with Pumping Over'. This last mechanical method has been the most successful and is much used for Australian Port-type wines. A trial of this method against the Pisa was conducted at Vargellas during the 1990 vintage by Andrew Birks (Lecturer in Wine Science at Charles Sturt University, NSW) and Miguel Sarmento (Escola Superior Biotecnologia, Oporto). Their conclusion reads: 'Maceration of premium Port wine grapes by *lagar* treading produces higher quality young Port wines with a better potential for development and selection into a vintage Port blend than the wines made from the static fermenter and pumpover method.'

The *Telegraph*'s own (our very own) Oz Clarke thinks that the 'good squashing and squoozing' of the pedal action is 'gentler, softer and squeezes out the aromas and colours'; mechanical methods make 'more aggressive Port'.

Alistair Robertson is quite unequivocal – he has no doubt but that treading produces better Port.

And me, what do I know? – I just like drinking the stuff.

[8]

I went to Dunvegan, on the Isle of Skye, to meet the Motor Yacht *Cefn Merlin* and have a few days getting all bronzed and sea-doggy-looking.

Merlin is a 51-foot, traditionally built boat: she combines the girth and comfortable build of a cook with the grace and speed of a countess (there are some pretty speedy countesses about). She is owned by an old friend of mine and skippered by the great Captain Rob Lapthorne, a Devon man whose skills were honed on Arctic survey vessels. There were just the three of us. It was not bronzing weather. It was raining, and a nice little south-westerly gale (Force 8) had been piling in from the Atlantic. *Merlin* had been snug in Loch Dunvegan for three days: time for some intensive research into Single Malts in the Dunvegan Hotel along with the statutory resident drunk.

It had been a long time since I had slept on a boat and how pleasant it was to snuggle down in the bunk with the gentle sound of water lapping against the side and the comfortable background hum of the 'genny'.

Next morning, the wind had moderated to a mere 6 to 7. The temperature had risen to the giddy heights of 12 degrees. I put my shorts and Ray-Bans deeper into the duffle bag. I wished that I had brought my shooting coat.

It was decided to make a run for it around the northern tip of Skye for the more sheltered waters of the Inner Sound. Rob warned that it would not be comfortable. It was a bit bumpy, but

Merlin is such a superb sea boat that she positively revelled in the Atlantic swell. It was a great pleasure to get the feel of a helm again and to revive a long-dormant skill. The most interesting bit was where the Little Minch lets rip between Rubha na h-Aiseig and Eilean Trodday. A look astern at the size of the following sea got the adrenaline pumping a bit.

We spent that night in the glassy calm of Upper Loch Torridon whose spectacular scenery was shrouded in mist.

So we went from loch to loch, eating a great deal of fish and spending cosy evenings dramming and holding tobacco parliaments in *Merlin*'s saloon, as the gales raged and the rain beat upon us and the yarns got more and more improbable.

We awoke to brilliant sunshine in Portree harbour on my last morning. *Mirabile dictu*, there was little wind. The play of light and shade on the hills as we motored gently down to the Kyle of Lochalsh was a true delight. We passed the site of the new bridge. No one whom I met was in favour of it. The local feeling was neatly summed up by the man who said: 'It won't be free and it will be an eyesore, but there's a few folk who will be lining their pockets out of the building of it.' I left *Merlin* with great regret. She is a truly lovely boat. Ah! the smell of the sea and the wind in your face and did you know that baked beans are forbidden on HM submarines?

[9]

To France and my old stamping ground of the Bourbonnais which is the profoundly rural centre of France. The English do not go much to this part of France these days, but that was not always so. The pretty, pastoral valley of the Besbre is full of little châteaux and fortified farmhouses built, as my French friends never tire of pointing out, for protection against the brutal and licentious English (the Scots were mostly fighting for the French) who trampled this area comprehensively. I suspect that few people in England today have heard of the Hundred Years War, but the French talk of it as though it were last week. Like the old lady who rounded on me at luncheon and pointed out that '*Les Anglais ont brûlés Jeanne d'Arc*', to which I had the presence of mind to reply: '*Bien sûr, mais les Français ont apportés les fagots.*'

I have written before of the wonderful oak forests in this part of France which are maintained on a sound and ancient coppicing system, whereby stands of beech grow amongst the oaks. The faster-growing beech acts as a forcer to oak saplings, making them grow straight. At the right stage the beech is cut and logged. Every house in this area has a huge (and neat) stack of weathering beech logs by the back door to feed the great wood-burning stoves.

I spent a morning wandering around a village market and dribbling over some of the wonderful goods on display – sausages, pâtés, cheeses, hams, fruit, vegetables, honey and fresh meat. Thereby hangs one of the vexed questions of our time – our export trade of live animals. Why not export carcases? One simple reason is that Alphonse, the local butcher, does not want a frozen carcase. He is an old-fashioned craftsman, who knows exactly what his very fussy customers want. He still does his own slaughtering, hanging and butchering and no one is going to tell him different. The French government knows that if it tried to implement all the EC directives on slaughterhouses, with all the prod-nosed zeal of MAFF, the blood on the floor would not all be animal.

We bought some delicious *saucissons* from a farmer who makes them on his farm from his own pigs. Did he have problems with Health Inspectors and such like Fonctionnaires? He was so amazed by this question that the fag fell out of his mouth and onto the *saucissons*: '*Monsieur*,' he said, '*en France le Gestapo est mort.*' What a pity that we cannot say the same en Grande Bretagne.

★

[10]

I did a leisurely train journey down through the middle of Middle England the other day. I speak of Middle England in the geographical sense as the phrase has become somewhat corrupted to mean (as I understand it) the sort of people who spend a lot of 'quality time caring, sharing, bonding' and lying down in front of cattle lorries – there might be a fortune to be made in selling T-shirts with ready printed tyre marks across them.

I like travelling by train, especially if I am not in a hurry. You can work, eat and sleep on a train. There are no bossy women telling you to sit up straight and fasten your seat belt.

The train took me through a bit of Middle England that I had never seen before. It was a nice old-fashioned train that ambled quietly along and fell asleep between the shafts when it stopped in stations. I was able to spend quality time with my pipe and look at the countryside. This was a countryside of water meadows and canals, where cows stood hock deep in grass in the shade of the willows. There was a ruined manor house with the crumbling walls covered in ivy – perhaps this was truly 'one of the ruins that Cromwell knocked about a bit'. There were several lonely churches sitting with their tumbled graveyards in the middle of fields, deserted by their villages after the Black Death.

It was nice to see that some of the old 'ridge and furrow' pastures still remain. I can remember when you could drive from Leicester to Stow-on-the-Wold on the Fosse Way (not too far to the west of my train) and never see a ploughed field. That was before the Common Agricultural Policy. A lot of this old pasture went down to grass in the agricultural slump of the 1870s. The really wide ridges were the ones ploughed by teams of oxen which needed a much wider turning circle than horses.

There were withy beds already showing the particularly fresh green of young willow. There were swans on the canal and a narrow boat full of hippies (or whatever they are called now). The gentle hills rolled away on either side of the track and the herd of fallow does nibbling away in the middle of a big arable field paid us no heed at all.

All in all it was a thoroughly pleasant and pleasing journey – Quality Time.

9. AUTUMN

[1]

The first morning's hunting of a new season and, although I have hunted nearly all my life, the magic is still there. The season proper does not start until November 1st, but hunting starts as soon as the harvest allows. Up in the hills, corn only appears in packets or in bottled form, so hounds can get started in August.

The autumn hunting is an early morning operation because once the day heats up, the scent dries. Very roughly, a fox's scent can be likened to minuscule drops of moisture. When the weather is cool and damp the scent will lie, but it quickly evaporates in the heat. Hounds hunt entirely by scent. On rough hill ground, it is very often possible for hounds to hit off the drag of a fox returning from his nocturnal foray and puzzle it out yard by yard into the bracken bed or cluster of rocks where he has lain up. Then there is the great roar of hound voices as the fox is put on his feet and then the first sight of the Red Rover as he slips across the heathery hillside. This moment never fails to make my back hairs stand up.

The meet was a cross-roads (well, sort of roads) high in the hills. There were about a dozen shepherds on their quadricycles, straight from their morning shepherding rounds, and some twenty cars. There was no hanging about. The Master just dropped the tail board of the lorry and hounds came boiling out, a mass of lemon, white and tan. Then the Master was on his quad and away.

Hounds were quickly spreading to a drag, but it came to nothing. The nearby brackens were blank but as soon as hounds entered the conifer plantation, they started speaking in earnest. The cry rose to a full-throated chorus. There was a fox afoot. The morning was cool and damp. There was a scent.

On the hill above the covert we could only wait and listen to the progress of the hunt, up and down the plantation. 'Whey, Man! yon's a ghrand soond altogether!' The tone of the cry changed: 'They're gan oot! they're oot beyant!' Hounds were out of the far side of the covert and 'gan like stoor!' (dust). Now was the moment to leap aboard the trusty quad and set out across the hill. Bump! crump! thump! across the bull snouts (grass tussocks), crash! bash! over the rocks hidden in the bonny, blooming heather (oh! the smell of blooming heather!), squelch! slurp! through the slimy peat hags (good thing I have put new tyres on). All the time, glimpses of hounds flying like a flock of gulls across the slope ahead, with snatches of cry coming back on the wind.

Hounds disappeared over the crest and when I got to the ridge (both shaken and stirred) they were hard about their work in some big, bouldery bracken beds in the next valley. They were into a litter of cubs here and there were foxes and hounds going all ways.

The only thing to do was to find a nice big rock to blunt the teeth of the bitter north wind (we were at about 1,800 feet up), light the pipe and sit and watch and listen to the sights and sounds that I love so well. We were hunting again.

Hounds caught four foxes that morning. Professor Stephen Harris of Bristol University has been described as a 'noted fox watcher'. In a recent newspaper article he is quoted as saying that it costs £70,000 for a hunt to catch a fox. He did not say on what he had based his calculations. After hunting, I put it to the Master that it had cost the hunt £280,000 to catch those four foxes. I will not tell you his exact reply, because it might upset the nice Professor. This hunt catches about two hundred foxes a season and its annual budget is in the reign of £30,000, so one does wonder where Prof. Harris bought his calculator.

The article also suggested a figure of 20,000 foxes killed by hunts (I have no idea). The Professor's calculator should then show that hunting pumps £1,400,000,000 per annum into the rural economy. My calculations of hunting as a rural industry had produced a more modest figure of £148 million, but then, I only just scraped O-level maths.

The newspaper article also claimed that foxes do not kill lambs. I put this to the assembled shepherds and I am certainly not going to tell you what they said.

[2]

Northumberland in a fine back end (autumn) is a place of quite extraordinary beauty. The variety of the colours that starts with the blooming of the heather and continues through the different shades of the dying bracken and the change of the leaf has been stunning. The early morning shepherding round has been a delight. Pulling on the boots in the boot room is always something of a trial. It doubles as the Rottweiler's bedroom and Rotties produce more gas than the North Sea. So it is a great moment when I open the back door and fill the lungs.

The wind has swept across the hills from the Irish Sea collecting the scent of heather, bracken and bent as it blows. There is a tang of frost in the air to sear the nostrils. The hills stand out clear and sharp in the hard northern light, with the cloud shadows racing across their multi-hued slopes. The collies come tumbling out of their kennels, racing and chasing around the yard whilst I get the quadricycle out of the shed. The cold wind makes me huddle into the high fleece collar of the old Irvine jacket.

We chug round each lot of stock. Those are some smart ewe lambs that Bob bought at Lazenby. There is a lame ewe amongst Jim's lot – I must telephone him at breakfast time. Jack's cows and calves are doing well and . . . ah! ha! what have we here? Mushrooms – big round saucers and coy little buttons. It does not take long to fill the plastic bag in my pocket. A slow drive down the side of the young plantation to admire the daily change of colours, then down to the pond – twelve mallard rise off it and the little moorhen scuttles into the reeds. A bit of fresh browse on a young tree and fresh roe buck slots – he is pushing his luck – but it is a lovely morning and there are mushrooms for breakfast. Away with care.

[3]

It is the little things that make life in the countryside so interesting and rewarding. Take for instance the fact that the swallows in the garage are now on their third brood – just as we had sighed with relief and taken the dust sheet off the car. I do not think that I can remember three broods in one year, but I suppose that it has been caused by the heat. I worry about the third brood and whether they will be strong enough to face the rigours of the autumn migration, but there is nothing that I can do to suppress the natural urges of swallows.

Some of my game hens have produced second broods this year. This is not the norm – they are usually content with rearing one family and do I hear cries of 'Amen to that!'

I set up a self-service feed hopper for the game hens. The hopper is activated by an inverted T-bar with a bright yellow crosspiece. If a bird pecks the T-bar a small shower of grain is released. My hens had never seen one of these contraptions before and we wondered how long it would take for them to suss it. The answer – in the case of one old hen with nine chicks – was about ten minutes. By now, most of them have cottoned on, but not the cock. He is much too grand for that sort of thing. He stands by the hopper and clucks until one of his wives comes and activates the widget for him and continues to do so until he has had enough. Woe betide any lesser fowl who tries to get a peck in whilst the boss is feeding. Of course, this is the natural order of things – we can learn many useful lessons for human society by studying the natural order.

[4]

I have long admired the writings of Ian Alcock and the drawings of his wife, Diana E. Brown (*see* page 186). The chance to meet them both and see the places which inspire the writings and drawings was not to be missed.

Ian is an Old Wykehamist, a hill farmer, a naturalist and, above all, a lover of deer. In 1974 he gave up a lucrative partnership in a City firm of stockbrokers and bought a farm in deepest Aberdeenshire. He wanted to put to the test his theories about farming in tune with nature. In his own words he became a 'peasant'.

Peasants or not, the Alcocks took a deal of finding; up a winding road that clambered through pine forests until it finally gave up at a somewhat deformed cattle grid and settled for just being a track. The track wound through scrubby birch woods until it reached the steading which (I am sorry, but it did) nestled below the hill. The welcoming committee consisted of turkeys, geese, a collie, two Vizlas, numerous hens, a row of interested ferret faces looking through the mesh of their palatial run and last, but not least, the Alcocks.

It was gone 6 pm when I arrived and after a quick cup of tea, Ian and I set out for the hill. Much of the farm is now an SSSI and has to be lightly stocked under the management agreement. This has allowed the growth of bracken and scrub to an extent that might make a truly commercial farmer wince. Ian does not mind; he has dug fifteen ponds since he has been there and planted shelter belts; it is a naturalist's paradise and a wonderful place for his beloved deer. It is also a wonderful place for an artist. Diana roams the hill on a pony with her sketch pad. Wildlife takes less notice of a human on a horse and this enables her to get closer to her subjects. The pony is accustomed to standing still whilst she sketches.

We climbed uphill through neck-high bracken and scrub until we came to an open space. Up went the binoculars. We saw the single hind first. Then a hind and calf appeared from the bracken, then two young stags and another hind and calf. The stags started play 'wrestling' with their antlers and we watched them in the gathering dark. Ian had said that he really needed to take one or two young stags to keep the population balance right. 'Take one if you like,' he said. I said that I thought that the light was not good enough. I think that we were both relieved. As we walked down, a stag started roaring on the hill.

Diana is a wonderful cook. The Alcocks eat their own beef and mutton. They take their own venison from the hill and wild mallard from the ponds. The vegetables come straight from the garden. That night we ate wonderful marbled Hereford X beef; real old-fashioned tasty stuff.

Next morning, I watched a hind and calf from my bedroom

window. We were maybe a little late getting on the hill and saw no more deer, although there were recent slot marks. We watched the buzzards soaring above, inspected some deer wallows, picked chanterelles under the birch trees, found the inside-out corpse of a rabbit that had been killed by a wild cat and watched a stoat working a drystone wall.

The climax of the visit came the next morning. This time it was still dark when we set out. We climbed the old green road until we got to the edge of the birches with some open hill in front. We saw the hinds first, about 400 yards away. Then the big stag appeared from some dead ground. He was uneasy. He was obviously watching something below him. He roared a challenge and a smaller stag appeared from some scrub and roared back. They quickly came together. For twenty minutes we watched them fight. This was no play; it was for real. We could hear the clash of the antlers clearly. Two more young stags appeared and circled the fighters who were by now sending up a great cloud of steam. At one stage, the younger contestant seemed to be winning, then the superior strength of the old beast told. The smaller beast turned tail and fled. The big stag, matted and black with sweat, stood roaring on the hill. He was the victor; or was he? The two little stags had sneaked off in the same direction as the hinds . . .

On the way back we saw a fine roe buck. It was a fitting end to a truly memorable visit to two remarkable people.

[5]

The New Forest is not new. It was new to William the Conqueror who made the area into a 'Forest', or Royal hunting preserve. Woe betide anyone who harmed the King's Deer. They were liable to have a few appendages (yes, including those) lopped off. The people responsible for the trimming up of offenders were the Verderers. The ancient court of Verderers meets regularly in

Lyndhurst to this day to 'protect and administer the Rights of Common over the unenclosed Forest'.

The New Forest is a massive recreational centre, with 8 million visitors every year. But behind the caravan parks, camp sites and wind-blown dog walkers, there is another, older forest, whose life goes on almost unnoticed by the transitory hordes. Some like to think of the New Forest as an untouched wilderness. This is not so. It is the way it is because of centuries of controlled burning, grazing, draining, timber production, scrub clearance and similar activities. The evolutionary process continues.

I went to look at the working Forest. For seventy years the Forestry Commission has managed the New Forest on behalf of the Crown. Arthur Barlow is the 'Deputy Surveyor'. He is the King of the New Forest, although he would deprecate the description, being a quiet and modest man. He was adamant that the Forest is 'a working place and not a theme park'. He regards his mandate as being to manage the Forest so as to maintain its traditional way of life, whilst catering for those who come for recreation and those for whom 'conservation' is the prime concern. The whole Forest is an SSSI, an SPA and a RAMSAR. With this situation, conflicts of interest are bound to arise and when they do Arthur Barlow is 'pig in the middle'.

There are ancient Common Rights in the Forest that are very likely Saxon in origin and which go with certain properties: 'Common of Pasture' for ponies, cattle, pigs, sheep and donkeys. The rights of 'pannage' when pigs may be loosed to feed on the acorns and beech mast. 'Marl' is the right to dig clay marl. 'Turbary' is the right to dig peat for fuel. 'Estover' is the right to firewood. These rights are the responsibility of the Verderers. They employ four Agisters whose job it is to ride the Forest and oversee the proper use of common rights and the welfare of the animals. It is the Agisters who organise the 'drifts', when the ponies are gathered in the autumn for worming, branding, tail marking and drafting for sale.

Jonathan Gerelli was the Agister in charge of the Burley Rocks Drift. About twenty riders had turned out to help. Most were

Commoners, but not all. Many people regard 'Colt Hunting' as a sport in itself, it being fast, exciting and dangerous. The scattered ponies are driven by a screen of riders into a fenced-in pound. The ponies gallop, twist and try to break back. They have to be ridden off and turned back to the herd. All this is done at speed over rough heather and broken ground; falls and smashed bones are regarded as part of the business. Very sensibly I remained on my feet, under the care of John Burry, the newly appointed 'Official Verderer' (the Head Man). The sun shone. The autumn colours were spectacular.

The riders had disappeared over the horizon. Then came some distant shouting. A line of horsemen appeared in the distance, with a bunch of about sixty ponies running in front of them. Those who were on foot lined out to guide them into the pound. But many of the old mares were not having it; they had been had before. Mares and foals broke to the side, in spite of determined efforts to turn them. 'Lost the bloody lot, an't us.' 'Reckon us better go down and get they.' But a large bunch had been pushed into the pound.

On a good drift they can bring in two hundred ponies in one drive, but on this day the ponies came in in small lots. This meant a lot of hard riding and some heated post mortems.

At last, the morning's drift was in the pound. After a brief pause for bait, the work began in earnest. Each Agister has a tail mark for his beat. This meant getting in amongst the milling ponies and cutting the appropriate notch in the tail hairs with a pair of shears; tricky work. All the ponies were wormed. The foals that were to remain on the Forest were then branded and registered. The ones to be sold (usually the colt foals) were separated and loaded onto the owners' trucks. The rest were then loosed back to the Forest. It had taken hours of sweaty, muddy and sometimes dangerous work. As one Commoner said: 'Ponies is a way of life.'

It was a fine morning for the meet of the New Forest Foxhounds at Longdown School. Besides the foxhounds there are the beagles and the buckhounds. The buckhounds still hunt the fallow buck as they have done for centuries. I had hoped to see them, but they stop hunting in October so as not to disturb the rut. It was a lovely morning to stride about the Forest listening to distant hound voices deep in some big coniferous Inclosures (sic).

In the afternoon, I visited Richard Stride. Richard is a Commoner, a Verderer and works for the Forestry Commission. The Strides are one of the very old Forest families, who were probably there before the Forest. Richard lives deep in the Forest with his family.

We all set off on a pony hunt, driving deep into the Forest, until we came to a meeting of riders where John Stride and his party were waiting. John is Richard's brother and partner. He is also huntsman to the buckhounds and renowned for his venery. The brothers particularly wanted to catch a cunning old mare who had so far managed to evade the main drifts.

'You want to watch they bloody pigs,' said John. It was the start of the pannage and pigs and their litters had been turned out into the Forest to feast on the acorns. Anyone who gets between a pig and her children is in for a sharp lesson in manners.

The pound we were working to was a beautiful thing with split oak rails. It was erected 'In memory of Agister Terry Jones 1991'. The pedestrians waited concealed behind trees at the run in to the pound, whilst the mounted hunters disappeared amongst the ancient trees and dying bracken. We could hear the buckhounds singing in their kennel. Two mares and their foals came racing into the pound and we ran to slip the bars behind them. 'They aren't the ones we want, but 'tis like hunting; good days and not so good days.' One mare and foal belonged to a brother-in-law. They were left in the pound for collection. The gate was tied, because 'do-gooders' sometimes turn them loose.

6 am and pitch dark: I was in a high seat with Keeper Robert Colin-Stokes. Robert is one of the twelve Keepers in the Forest. A big part of their job is deer control, but they are also notable naturalists. Robert's speciality is snakes. We were sitting for a buck. We sat still and silent for two hours whilst the dawn broke

over the Forest: nothing. People know where the deer ought to be, but no one tells the deer. We saw plenty of them later in the morning: a herd of red deer with a fine stag, a sika hind and a calf, a roe doe and plenty of fallow, including a 'prime' buck on a rutting stand ('love nest'). These stands suffer greatly from interference by walkers who all think 'it can't matter if I go and have a look', but sixty persons all thinking the same can cause a problem. As Robert said: 'How would they like being watched when they were doing it?'

Arthur Barlow invited me to attend a Drainage Meeting with representatives of the Forestry Commission, Keepers, Commoners, Verderers and conservation bodies. Drainage is a hot potato. Commoners worry that lack of drainage spoils their grazing, hard won over the centuries. The Conservationists worry about anything that interferes with the doubtful husbandry of Mother Nature. 'I cannot agree with that!' is a phrase much used. It is not surprising that feelings sometimes run high. Arthur Barlow's benign good humour is often in demand.

The New Forest is loved by those who live and work there and by those who recreate there, but from different viewpoints. This dichotomy was neatly demonstrated by an incident which happened during my visit. A jogger got himself between a sow and her piglets and got himself comprehensively bitten in the bum.

Proper management of the Forest is vital if it is not be loved to death. At the moment it seems to work well. There are those who would wish a full National Park status for the New Forest, but as the old saying goes: 'If it's not broken, don't try to mend it.'

[6]

The harvest is mostly finished in this part of England and the stubble fields are full of huge round straw bales waiting to be loaded and carried away to stack and barn. I used to love loading and stacking big bales. I am sure that those of you who have seen the things are now making complimentary noises about my massive physique. Well, thank you very much but, whilst my body is indeed splendid, it does not attempt to lift those socking great things. Oh dear me, no. These days it is all done from the seat of a tractor.

There are various gadgets that you can play with, but the main things are the Spike and the Jaws. The spike is a long tapered spike mounted on the fore-end loader of the tractor. The bale needs to be on its side. Then you line up the tractor, whack up the revs (you can imagine the machine pawing the ground and snorting), lower the fore end so that the spike points at the middle of the bale and CHARGE!! BULLSEYE!! you impale the bale. Then with a flick of the hydraulics you lift it high in the air, as though it were a dragon on a lance, and bear it to lorry, wagon or stack.

I had a bale grab which is altogether sneakier. The grab is like the hydraulically operated jaws of a dragon with great steel teeth. With this, you sidle up to an unsuspecting sunbathing bale, then with a flick of a lever, the jaws encircle it, the great teeth sink into it and up it goes.

There is another use for a bale grab that does not appear in the manufacturer's blurb. A man of my acquaintance farms near a beauty spot and has a great deal of trouble with the Great British Public leaving gates open. One day, having just very carefully sorted some lambs into two lots, he saw a school party march through one of his gates and leave it open so that the sorted lambs were reunited. He drove across in his tractor to remonstrate with the teacher and got called a 'F—g peasant'. He told me afterwards that it is quite amazing how fast a sedentary creature like a teacher can cross a field with a bale grab snapping at his backside.

★

143

[7]

The Strange Behaviour of Birds – no, no, no – not that sort – not much fluttering around me these days, I can tell you. Mike works in the forests and is a great naturalist. I saw him out hunting the other day and he was telling me something that had us both beat. He had been watching the strange behaviour of rooks on some Scots pines. The birds were going for the green cones and he said that they were going through the most amazing contortions to get them. By definition the cones tend to be out on a limb and a rook is a biggish bird. The rooks were making landings on very fragile branches. They were obviously desperate to get the green cones and they had to be green and growing – any cones on the ground were ignored. Once a rook had plucked a cone it flew off with it – any explanations, please?

And while you are at it, please explain this one. There is a rookery in the wood behind the house and as I look out of the office window, I can see the incoming rooks. Often they are carrying twigs in their beaks. In the spring they would be nest building, but what are they doing in October? Rooks are very interesting birds with a complicated social structure, but what does the twig carrying betoken?

NOTE Answer came there none to that question. Pity.

[8]

The high (16 feet) seat was sited so as to give a good view over a young conifer plantation. The trees were at the stage when they were very vulnerable to damage from browsing deer. Deer like to nibble fresh young growth and who can blame them? The trouble is that young trees that have been browsed may die. At best they may grow misshapen which means that the tree never achieves its aesthetic or commercial potential. So deer numbers have to be controlled. The high seat is one of the tools of the woodland stalkers' trade. By being up a height, he can look down into the plantation and see deer that would not be visible from ground level. It also means that the angle of the shot is downwards and therefore into the ground. This means that it is a safe shot. The stalker always has to be mindful of the Great British Peregrinating Public who might take a dim view of a 150 grain bullet up its collective Kagool.

The GBPP might bear this fact in mind before it succumbs to the Bambi Syndrome and starts sawing halfway through the uprights of high seats with a view to damaging the stalker. The GBPP would not dream of doing such a thing? May Heaven preserve your innocence and your Kagool.

All this is something of a digression as this is not about deer, but foxes. The nice thing about sitting high and quiet is the other woodland life that one sees, especially at dawn and dusk. This is when the woodland stalker operates, deer being crepuscular feeders.

On this particular evening, the pheasants were waddling in from the stubbles, rather like members of a Livery Company after a very good dinner. A flicker of moving red caught my eye and there was a well-grown fox cub looking for his supper. For some twenty minutes, I watched as he stalked and pounced at various birds. I marvelled at his grace, but not at his skill which needed a bit of honing. Perseverance is a great quality. At last, a young cock disappeared into a thicket with the cub at his tail feathers. There was a loud squawk and then silence: dinner had been served.

What about the deer? I saw none, but the evening was not over. As I was driving away up through the pitch-black woodland, the van slid off the muddy ride and into the even muddier ditch. The 4-wheel drive availed me nothing. It was a tractor job. As I waited for succour, the stars were burning brightly in the still, frosty sky.

The owls were hooting in the wood and from far across the water meadows came the sound of bell ringing practice in the village on the hill: not a bad way to spend an evening but, my goodness, that whisky did taste good when I finally got home.

And, finally . . .

My old friend Dougal, the Sage of Glen Bhollach (pronounced vollack), spent all his working life as a shepherd and stalker. This meant being out in all the various kinds of weather (mostly wet) that the Western Highlands might produce. Dougal would come in soaked from the hill and stand in front of the old open range, revolving slowly until dry. It is not surprising that he now has what he calls the 'arthuritis' which is making his hands close like claws. They were getting bad when I saw him recently and I suggested that he consult the doctor.

'Doctors? I have no need of doctors, Man!! When a hand gets bad I put it on the table and draw it out as far as I can, then I get a muckle heavy book and clatter it flat.'

10. NOAH'S DISCIPLES

[1]

Once upon a time there was a bull terrier called Lucy who lived in Bexleyheath, a cat called Fluffy and a small bird whose identity has not been disclosed.

Lucy found Fluffy in the act of killing a bird in her (Lucy's) garden. Lucy chased the cat and killed it. Seven policemen (*seven*, for Heaven's sake!) came and arrested Lucy on the grounds that she was 'out of control'.

Let us consider this with a little logic. It has been said that it was Lucy's instinct to pursue and kill the cat. Her instinctive reaction got her arrested under the 'Dangerous Dogs Act' – the sole political memorial of the Home Secretary Kenneth 'Mad Dog' Baker – and facing a possible death sentence.

Fluffy the cat was also following its instinct when it set out to total some hapless songbird. However, it could be said that Fluffy was also 'out of control' at the time of the killing and, whilst out of control, the cat committed an offence under Section 1 (1) of the Wildlife and Countryside Act 1981 in that 'it is an offence intentionally to kill, injure or take any wild bird'. Anyone who lets a cat loose with the certain knowledge that it will do just that must be an 'accessory after the fact', and it would seem to follow that both Fluffy and its elderly lady owner should be arrested and charged (by as many plods as the Met deems necessary) under this Act. Fluffy's arrest would have to be posthumous, but the owner should face the full rigours of the law. After all, justice is blind and if a dog can be out of control and its owners held responsible for its actions, then why not a cat?

Why not a cat, especially? There is a fascinating report published by Dr N. C. Fox, BSc, CEd, PhD, called 'Aspects of Killing Wild Animals in Britain'. Dr Fox makes the point that the estimated 7.5 million cats in Britain kill 75 million birds and 135 million mammals every year. Cats are wanton killers and, as most are extremely well fed by their doting animal-loving owners, they have no need to kill. Dr Fox makes the point that 'simply reducing predation by cats during the sensitive breeding months of April to July could reduce wildlife deaths by 100 million per year . . .' How many of those who write passionate letters about 'the plight of our songbirds' are cat owners?

I suspect that most cat owners know that their cats kill, but choose to ignore the fact. It follows that any persons who allow their cat to roam are 'accessories after the fact' that the Wildlife and Countryside Act will be broken due to their lack of control. I trust that the Metropolitan Police and all other police forces will take cognisance of this flagrant flouting of the law and that we can look forward with confidence to the mass arrests of cat owners

148

– after all, the Met has got to do something with the time that it cannot be bothered to spend investigating break ins and car thefts.

A coda – as I wrote this piece a Metropolitan Police dog was killing a raven at the Tower of London. This dog was undoubtedly 'out of control' but I understand that the Met has no plans to arrest it and I do not suppose that the ravens are 'wild' birds within the meaning of the WL&C Act. However, they are the property of the Crown and essential to the maintenance of the Monarchy. At the very least, the Met Commissioner should be charged with 'damaging Crown property'. At worst, he should be charged with High Treason, loaded with chains and banged up in the Tower – *Quis custodiet ipsos custodes.*

[2]

I have written previously about Jonathan Brock, my tame badger, and his famous rout of the Women's Institute (in *The Cheviot Ranter*). Since then there have been several letters asking what happened to Jonathan. It is a sad story.

The day came in my life when I put my possessions in a feed sack, stuffed a bit of bread and cheese in my pocket and set out to seek my fortune. It was decided that Jonathan should go and live with the local doctor. He had children and Jonathan was very fond of children. I received regular bulletins and the arrangement seemed to be working well. I used to go to see him on my home visits.

The doctor had some old stables in his back yard, with outside stone steps leading to a loft. Jonathan had his bed in the loft and when he was not rooting about in the orchard, he liked to curl up on the top of the steps and watch what was going on. That was where I found him, that last time. He had grown into a biggish boar, but was still pleased to see me. I sat on the steps with him for about an hour whilst he wriggled and chittered around me, investigating my pockets, prodding me with his nose, climbing onto my lap to have his tummy scratched and trying to arrange himself round my neck as had been his wont. He came with me to the yard gate when I left.

That was the last time that I saw him. A few weeks later I got a letter to say that Jonathan had been poisoned. It was deliberate. Poor old Jonathan Brock.

[3]

'Oh Conservation! what rubbish is purveyed in thy name!' Conservation is one of those buzz words that everybody uses, but few people can actually define. 'Cruelty' is another. Next time someone says that you are cruel, ask them to define cruelty. It is a guinea to a gooseberry that they will shuffle their feet, look shifty and say, 'Well, you know, cruel – you know.' And well you may, but do they? Press them on this point and they will get cross. At this point suggest that they go and look the word up in the dictionary. They will get crosser still.

As I am bored with people bandying 'Conservation' about, I looked it up in my well-thumbed *Chambers Dictionary*. One of the excellent Mr (or Ms for all I know) Chambers' definitions is 'something preserved, as fruits in sugar'. 'Fruits in sugar' seems as good a definition of many self-styled 'Conservationists' as could be wished for. My beard and whiskers! some of them do talk nonsense.

There was a recent newspaper report headed 'Mammals in Decline'. Amongst these mammals that are said to be 'stooping or condescending' (*Chambers*) are the brown hare and the badger.

Those of us who have our being and labour in the countryside (as opposed to those who tittup about it in highly unsuitable shoes that fall off in muddy gateways and have to be retrieved by farmers in black wellies) know that the badger population has exploded in recent years. I like badgers and like watching them. They are the most fascinating animals. I probably see more badgers than most people as I am often out and about when they are. It is probable that most people never see them, badgers being largely nocturnal, and this makes it easier for them to believe that the animals are scarce. Badgers are not scarce; indeed, they are reaching plague proportions in certain parts of the country and I use the word plague advisedly. There have been suspicions for a long time amongst dairy farmers that badgers are carriers of tuberculosis. As I understand it, MAFF carried out tests in various parts of the West of England to check on this. They seem to have been very coy about publishing the results. This coyness has led to a growing suspicion that there may indeed be a connection between badgers and bovine TB, but that the Ministry regards this as such a conservational hot potato that it is sitting on it. This cannot be a very comfortable thing to do with a hot potato. Until the Ministry grasps the nettle (another uncomfortable metaphor), rumour will continue to spread to the detriment of the badger's reputation.

In this same article it is stated that 50,000 badgers are killed on the roads every year. I wonder how anyone can possibly know this figure. A badger killed on the road is a rare thing to see. It is very probable that badgers are hit by cars and, being extremely tough animals, crawl away to die but I have no evidence of that and neither does anybody else. Beware of all statistics relating to animals; the numbers are usually picked with a pin. I might as well say that 87% of all conservationists eat Dutch veal. Disprove that if you can.

Now let us look at the hare: I was only remarking to myself the other day how many hares there seem to be about this year. The brown hare has undoubtedly benefited from the increase in set-aside and increased tree planting (as I know to my cost). There have been two recent surveys to *estimate* the hare population of Britain. One survey was done by the Joint Nature Conservation Committee, whatever that may be. This survey estimated the population to be between 680,000 and 954,000. This certainly shows a drop from the estimated figure of 4 million in 1900, but where that figure came from only the JNCC knows – however, see above.

The Game Conservancy Trust has also done a Hare Survey. It must be emphasised that the two surveys used different counting methods. The GCT has the hare population at 'between 1–2 million'.

I have no doubt that the argument will continue to rage, that population figures will be plucked out of the air to support various theories and that, in blissful ignorance of all this fuss, brown hares and badgers will continue to thrive – in spite of conservationists.

[4]

Rooks are remarkable birds with a definite social structure. I was sitting on a hill overlooking some fields and a wood where there is a rookery. It was just coming on to dusk. With the dusk came wave after wave of rooks who settled in the big field on my left. They must have numbered several thousand. It is no exaggeration to say that the field was black with birds. The noise was quite incredible. This meeting/debriefing is a normal part of corvine behaviour, but I had never seen one on this scale before. There they stood, bobbing and bowing and cawing at each other. Every so often the ones farthest from the wood took flight and landed in at the head of the meeting so that the whole mass appeared to be rolling across the field. The old men say that this is when the rooks discuss their plans for the next day, although how they hear what is being said must remain a mystery. As the crepuscular shade deepened, sections of the mass began taking off and settling into the trees. Within ten minutes the field was empty. The noise in the trees rose to a grand climax, then gradually faded away as darkness deepened.

I have known human meetings that generated as much noise, but few of them have ended with such exemplary order and despatch. We have much to re-learn from nature. How I disagree with the nice man from the League Against Cruel Sports who told me that human beings can only be improved by suppressing their natural urges. It is because we disregard nature that we, and our planet, are in so much trouble.

[5]

Let us go all Scottish – 'Many a mickle makks a muckle' (little things add up) and 'Muckle work and mickle woo' [wool] the De'il said as he clipped the soo' [sow]' (no one likes working hard for nothing). I was reminded of this when talking to a friend who farms near a beauty spot and is blessed with a public footpath through one particular field. The friend has a beef suckler herd (cows and calves). The herd is seldom put in the field with the footpath for two reasons.

The first is that many people think that 'public' applies to their dogs as well as them, so I think that a warning is in order – NEVER TAKE YOUR DOG INTO A FIELD WITH COWS AND CALVES!!!! Beef cows are docile on the whole, except when they have calves at foot, then atavistic urges take over. If they had ever measured the Hop, Skip and Jump that I once made with a maternal Galloway cow on my tail, I would be world champion now. I know that Dear Old Fido has never offered violence to anything other than a teddy bear and I am quite sure that you have him on a lead but remember that, as far as a suckler cow is concerned, Fido is a WOLF seeking to convert her child into *plat du jour*.

The other reasons for the cows not being put in the field with the footpath are little ones – lots of little ones: sandwich packets, lager cans, plastic bottles, condoms (usually used), burger boxes, broken glass – all of this and much more has to be collected before the cows may safely graze. Many a mickle makks a muckle – so please take your muckle home with you.

[6]

Little Cass has gone. He came to us nineteen years ago – a small, four-legged ball of fluff in a Heinz Baked Bean box. He was a birthday present for my wife and cost me £8.

Little Cass's proper name was Cassoulet. His mother was a very smart, pedigree Dandie Dinmont who had hopped over the fence with a Cairn × Yorkshire Terrier × Wire-Haired Dachshund – thus he was a mixture based on sausage. He was a dog of immense character and most of it unfortunate – he was greedy, scruffy, obstinate and determinedly randy: we loved him dearly. His great passion in life was rabbiting. He would spend all day every day in pursuit of the elusive rabbit. His forays would take him far from home, leaving his owners fuming and worried about the bloody little dog. He was once missing for three days. The countryside was scoured. The Gendarmerie was on full alert. On the fourth morning I came down to find him curled up on the doorstep, a tangled mass of burrs and dried mud. 'Oh you bloody little dog,' I said as I picked him up and he licked my nose.

If he was tired and far from home, he would go and sit in the middle of a road until someone picked him up and brought him home in comfort, or took pity on him and bore him home with them. Many a telephone call has brought me raging to my van and always I would find the little swine rumped up by someone's fire, being petted and fed on chocolate cake. When we moved to Northumberland he had his own rabbit warren, and there he would spend long days baying and digging. I do not think that he ever actually managed to catch a rabbit. There was the celebrated occasion when Cass was proceeding west along one side of a wire fence, snuffling on the line of a rabbit, and he actually met the rabbit going east on the other side of the fence – they totally ignored each other.

The last time that he went AWOL, he was arrested for sitting in the middle of the A697 and causing a traffic jam and was banged up at Rothbury Police Station. We could hear his anguished wails (he had a particularly ghastly wail) long before we got there: 'He's a dear little chap,' said the Sergeant. 'He's a bloody little dog,' said the Wife and I in unison.

In the last year of his life he became deaf, nearly blind and his poor old mind had wandered, but then in human terms he was c. 130 years old. He was not suffering, just very old. It was my wife who took the hard and correct decision and called the vet. The little dog slipped away quietly in his own bed. He was a bloody little dog and we miss him terribly.

[7]

There is no doubt that shepherds care deeply for their sheep. You cannot work with sheep unless you like them and are deeply conscious of their welfare. There is a practical aspect to this: a well-cared-for sheep is most likely to make a profit. Therefore, I know that I am not alone amongst shepherds in worrying about what happens to sheep once they have gone through the farm gate. I would like to see all lambs and draft ewes slaughtered as close to home as possible. This would minimise the stress on the animal, which in turn would improve the quality of the meat for the consumer. This has become more difficult because of over-zealous application of EC rules by our own bureaucrats, rules which every other EC country agrees to but never enforces. The zealots of MAFF like to add a few flatulent restrictions of their own as well. All this has brought about the disappearance of many local abattoirs. This means that sheep may now have to travel many hours to be slaughtered. The last load of lambs that

I sold in Northumberland were slaughtered in Dover for the export trade.

Some 45% of our lamb now goes for export and this important market is growing. Of this export trade c. 25% depends on the export of live animals. There are rules and regulations about the transport of live animals and where these rules are followed, the process is tolerable if not likeable. Most exporters are responsible people with reputations to maintain, but there are those in every business who seek to increase profits by cutting corners and, in this case, causing unacceptable suffering to the animals. No shepherd wants this. The life of a lamb is short, let it be as merry as possible.

[8]

There has been proper concern in the media about allegations of the illegal killing of raptors (hawks/owls) in various parts of the country. I say a proper concern, but it is also proper that people started to consider the effects that blanket protection of certain species might have on the balance of nature.

Take a for instance: here in the Borders there is increasing concern about the explosion of the goshawk population from a zero base. There is also concern about how they came to be here. Some say that sparrowhawks' nests were robbed and the eggs replaced with goshawks' eggs. Others say that the original goshawks were released into the wilds. A regular correspondent says that he has seen a letter from a 'Conservation Body' stating that ninety goshawks were released into the wild last year. The robbing of raptors' nests and the releasing of raptors into the wild without a licence are both illegal acts under the Wildlife and Countryside Act, but I have yet to hear of any prosecutions pending. However it was done, the goshawks are here. I often see them in the woods and marvel at the way they weave through the branches. The irony and the sadness is that the area chosen for the goshawk 'experiment' is also one of the last remaining strongholds of the red squirrel for whom goshawks are a matter of death. The natural balance cannot support uncontrolled predator species. No one doubts the good intentions of 'Conservation Bodies', but what a pity that they do not *think*. Why did they not put the goshawks where they would eat those beastly *grey* squirrels (more properly tree rats)? One day the nettle of controlling protected species will have to grasped and people will not feel the need to break the law. I watch my red squirrels with renewed pleasure and some sadness: they will soon be gone.

11. ALL MY PROCLIVITIES
ARE SPORTING

[1]

NOTE The following article was written in 1993 when both Newcastle and Brentford were in the First Division, and Kevin Keegan was still manager; at that time, too, standing was still allowed in the terraces.

'Ye kna wit ye are? Ye're a—vorgin (please note: all—should be assumed to be the 'F word'). The place was the Gallowgate terraces of St James's Park; the occasion the match between

Newcastle United and Brentford; the reason for the outburst the fact that I had just disclosed that this was the first football match that I had ever attended. For those about me there was no world without football and Newcastle United was the centre of their universe. I was taken in hand by Johnny Cannell and his six-year-old son, Philip. Johnny and Philip attend every home game and Johnny travels away as often as he can. Philip wants to play for Newcastle.

All around us the stands and terraces started to fill up, whilst heavily amplified rock music blasted the eardrums. Black and white striped shirts, scarves and hats were the order of the day.

At the far end of the ground the Brentford fans were corralled in a tiny enclosure, separated by strong fencing and a line of policemen from the Leazes terraces, whose occupants were making it plain that they took a dim view of visiting supporters. Gallowgate was loud in support: 'Cut their—b—s off!'

The music was now being jockeyed by Mr Tim Healey, the comic actor. Between records he told jokes. Mr Healey's jokes had the effect of reducing the stadium to total silence: no mean feat. 'What a—bummer,' said a voice.

Well-muffled players appeared on the pitch to roars of applause and started doing warm-up exercises which seemed to have all the grace of defecating dogs. When they were apparently warm enough, they disappeared.

Mr Healey wanted us all to sing a song called 'Hello! hello! we are the Geordie Boys'. It seemed to consist of constant repetition of that line and a list of players' names.

The now unmuffled teams re-appeared to heavy booing for Brentford and volcanic cheering for the Lads. Philip started chanting 'We won the cup'. The whistle blew and we were off.

There is no doubt that if you want to experience the raw power and emotion that football engenders, then you should go and stand on the terraces. Locked in shoulder to shoulder and front and back you are surrounded by people for whom life is probably not a bed of roses, people for whom their local team provides a sheet anchor of belief and worship in a dreary world. This is why winning is so important; who wants to worship losers? Football is a tribal conflict. The cries of 'Brakk his—leg!', 'Howway ye poofy bastard, put yer knee in his nuts' do not suggest Olympian ideals. The Gallowgaters go to watch football to be made to feel good and for a good emotional catharsis.

'Howway, Ref, ye donnered ard boogger!'

'Bury the—bastid!'

'Neeeewcassel! Neeeewcassel! howway lads, get the —s!'

Brentford was defending our end during the first half. The goalkeeper was wearing a top of many colours. A voice behind said that it looked like 'my Saturday night spew'.

Then Newcastle scored: eruption: earthquake: thousands of beer-fogged voices bayed; arms flailed; a heavily tattooed arm kept thumping me on the shoulder. The feeling of ecstasy was contagious and I leaped about and bellowed too. Apart from excitement, it would not be good policy to be cool and detached on the Gallowgate, when the Lads had scored a 'magic —g goal'.

The tannoy announced the search for 'Mr Organ', a missing member of a Norwegian party. The Gallowgaters made hay.

The game went on. Someone at the back of the terrace let off some kind of smoke bomb. Two enormous policemen forced their way through the crowd. The incident was filmed from the front. We all waved to the police video.

Newcastle seemed to be slowing down. The players seemed to be doing lots of complicated footwork and beautiful passing without actually getting anywhere near the goal. The terrace accused the team of trying to 'walk it in'. Those who had been gods, a few short moments before, were now 'poofy bastids'. The whistle blew for half time.

I shook hands with Johnny and Philip. Philip wished me 'all the best' and the same to them and my thanks.

I was whisked away round the pitch by Gordon Graham, the very imposing Supervisor of Stewards. Some of the comments from the stands at our passing were definitely slanderous. Gordon just laughed and shrugged his massive shoulders: it was all part of the job.

It was now time to enter the rarefied atmosphere of the Directors' Box, high at the top of the stand. Here was a rather more refined atmosphere and a welcome cup of coffee from my 'minder', Sharon Fletcher, the Chief Executive's charming secretary.

My seat was high up above the halfway line, with a panoramic view of the packed stands and terraces (30,006 people). Here I was amongst 'the Suits' and an apparently much more muted atmosphere, but . . . In the second half Newcastle scored four more goals and had one disallowed. As the tension mounted, so did the baying of the crowd. The infectious tension began to peel the veneer from those about me until the magic moment when, after the waiting agony of 'injury time', the final whistle went and pandemonium reigned as the teams came off. Newcastle was obviously 'over the moon' and the crestfallen Brentford 'gutted'.

Now was the time for the great and the very good to be invited to the Chairman's Office. Sir John Hall was rumoured to be in a good mood, as well he might be. Sir John is a legend on Tyneside. A lean quiet courteous man, but with eyes that miss nothing and tell you why his moods are a matter of remark amongst his staff. He certainly runs a tight ship and this shows in the cheerful efficiency of all the staff at St James's. Sir John is a true lover of the game and regards his players not just as footballers but as a power for good on Tyneside. 'They are looked upon as gods.' He feels that if Kevin Keegan and the Lads form up and say 'don't do this' (as it might be taking drugs) then people will not do it. And there was me thinking that football was just a game. Ah well, even 'vorgins' have to learn and I am very grateful to all of Newcastle United for such a pleasant defloration.

'Five one! five one! five one! Howway the Lads!'

★

[2]

What is a musher? It is the driver of a team of huskies. Not many
people know that. I did not know either until last weekend when
the Siberian Husky Club of Great Britain (recognised by the
Kennel Club in 1977) held a 'Snow Rally' in the vasty deeps of
Kielder Forest, Northumberland. If there is snow to be had it is
likely to be found there, in the desolate watershed of the North
Tyne. This year the weather obliged. On the Saturday there
was a good covering of snow. On the Sunday the snow was
disappearing in the sort of bone-chilling fog and cold south-
easterly rain that Northumberland specialises in. However, there
was still enough snow for sleds to be used, rather than the Heath
Robinsonesque tricycle 'rigs' that are used when there is no snow.
A rig is a lightweight, tubular steel tricycle with a standing platform.

It is probable that most people in this country have never seen
huskies in action, so a little background is called for. Huskies have
been pulling sleds for man in the frozen northern wastes for at
least 4,000 years. For the indigenous inhabitants of the snowy
wildernesses, sled dogs were the only means of travelling large
distances to hunt and trap and trade. Man and his dog team are
still important in remote snowbound areas. But what purpose do
dog teams have in the temperate British Isles? Simple—they are
fun.

The huskies could be heard long before they came in sight.
Their howling added to the desolation of the wild, white forest.
Huskies do not bark, they howl. The lonely road behind Kielder
Castle, bounded by dark dripping sitka spruce, was lined with
somewhat battered vans. Each vehicle was surrounded by a clutter
of sleds, harness, dog bowls and general paraphernalia. There
were huskies everywhere, tied to vans, tethered to trees, or curled
up in the back of the vans.

The Siberian Husky, as everybody present (some of the national
membership of c.1,000) took great pains to point out, is the only

true husky – pure-bred and recognised by the Kennel Club. There are other types such as 'Malamutes' and 'Eskimo dogs' which are, well, not quite, you know. Huskies are splendid dogs, thick coated with rather lupine heads and bushy waving tails. The bitches weigh in at c. 30–40 lbs and the dogs c. 50–60. The first pair of Siberians arrived in this country in 1968. The husky is docile and friendly and good in the house, but it is a working dog and it loves to pull and run – it really loves to run.

The number of entries (c.30) at Kielder had been reduced by the blizzard on the previous Friday night. So it was nothing like the recent rally at Aviemore where 120 teams competed, but even so mushers had fought their way through from all over the country, from Scotland to Hampshire. One team had come all the way from Plymouth.

When I arrived, the 6-dog teams were starting. The course had been shortened because of the ground conditions, and was a c. 5½-mile loop around the head of a valley on a forestry track. The dogs wore nylon webbing body harnesses. Each pair was coupled together at the collar. A central trace (the 'gang line') ran down between the dogs and was attached to each dog at the collar and at the rear of the harness. It was then attached to the front of the sled. The sleds were of ancient pattern, about 8 feet long and weighing less than 40 pounds. They were made of white ash, hickory or birch. The musher balanced on the rear of the two runners, when he was not running himself.

At the start the huskies waited, but not patiently – they wanted to RUN! Each pair was held by a helper and the sled was firmly tethered to a steel post. The mushers went round talking to their dogs, often kneeling down to embrace them and whisper to them. These people really love their dogs.

'Thirty seconds,' called the starter. The musher went back to his sled. The dogs were howling and straining. 'Ten – nine – eight –' The howling became acute: they knew. '*Zero!*' They were off. The musher, running behind the sled, emitted wild holloas of encouragement. When the sled was running well, he leaped onto his precarious footholds. It was exciting stuff.

Between the 6-dog and the 4-dog competitions, Penny Knock (Forest Enterprise Recreation Ranger) took me out onto the course on the back of her quadricycle. The top end of the loop was clear felled and so I could watch the teams uphill on one side, round the sharp bend at the top and back down the other side. They were fit, those mushers. They spent a lot of time running on the uphill gradients. You could hear them coming. The mushers were always cheering on, talking to and encouraging their dogs. A running dog team is a stirring sight. Even towards the end of the course, the dogs were keen as ever and, as the finish line came in sight, the helpers were there to shout and yell encouragement.

Husky racing is fun and fascinating. Dogs and persons enjoy themselves and each other – them ol' mushers and them ol' dogs. Boy, they just love to run.

[3]

The greyhound has the fastest acceleration of any animal on earth – bar none. The wild brown hare has agility, stamina and local knowledge. The interaction between the two has been fascinating Man (and Woman) since ancient times. This is coursing.

The Waterloo Cup is the Blue Riband of the coursing world. It is run every year at Altcar, near Southport. The Cup was started in 1836 by William Lynn, owner of the Waterloo Hotel in Liverpool. He also started a steeplechase at nearby Aintree which a local paper dubbed 'The Grand National'.

Lord Leverhulme's Altcar estate is run and farmed with coursing and hare preservation in mind – no poaching, no sprays that might harm hares – 'The hares live in a hares' paradise, in return for which they may have to run like **** once a year' – no hare is coursed more than once and many not at all.

Who goes coursing? At the Call Over, the night before the

meeting, there was a truly Corinthian mix of Swell and Rough. Suits chatted with leather jackets; monocles compared notes with pigtails and earrings. The one thing that they all seemed to have in common was a love of greyhounds and coursing.

The Waterloo is run over three days, Tuesday, Wednesday and the final on Thursday – each day on a different coursing ground.

Tuesday was at the Withins. The flat fenland of Lancashire was very wet after days of rain. The meet was due for 0900, but was delayed as vehicles struggled with the conditions. The weather looked ominous (last year, the meeting was snowed off), but the day cleared, with a biting, drying wind.

On one side of the coursing ground were the car parks. On the other, a raised banking where spectators can stand. Clothing was 'rural sensible'. In the conditions (and after the night before) an 0900 Bloody Mary from the boot of a friendly Range-Rover seemed a bonzer idea – coursing people are extremely hospitable.

The hares are driven into a large expanse of plough ground at the end of the grass coursing area. The art of the beating is to ensure that the hares have time to settle and are not under pressure to break in a mass flush – remember, these are truly wild hares. As a hare breaks from the plough, her (all hares are 'she') instinct is to run down the open grass of the coursing area. At the plough end of the area is a three-sided canvas hide (the shy) where the slipper waits with the two dogs in the heat.

Garrett (Gary) Kelly has been a licensed slipper since 1966. His job is first to judge whether the hare is suitable. If the hare looks poor or is not moving well, it is ignored. The hare should pass within 30 yards of the shy and be moving straight. When the hare is 80–100 yards in front of him he will run forward with the dogs and when he is sure that the dogs are 'sighted' they are slipped. Unfair? The hare is an animal bred for flight – she has 80% rear vision, can turn in her own length at speed and has far more stamina than a greyhound. Each dog wears a white or red collar. In general terms (the scoring system is complicated) the mounted judge awards points for speed and the dog's ability to make the hare turn. His decision is marked by waving a red or white handkerchief. The average course takes 40 seconds and once the hare reaches the rough grass at the end of the coursing ground, the dogs are unsighted and the course is over. On average, one hare in eight is killed. Out of sixty-four courses on the Tuesday, I only saw three hares killed and it is a quick end.

I spent some time in the shy and was fascinated by the skill of the slipper. He judged each hare as it came – 'No, she looks weak, no back on her' – the dogs saw the hare and strained – no slip. The slipper also has to know the dogs and judge their strengths relative to each hare. 'This looks a nice hare' – the hare lolloped past – the dogs sighted it – Gary waited – judged the moment – ran forward with the straining dogs – snapped the automatic release which frees both collars simultaneously – the course was on!

What wonderful movers those dogs are! See that black bitch powering on! she's upsides of the hare! the hare jinks! the dog almost comes down in its attempt to turn. Now the other dog turns the hare, but she is away into the rough grass at the end and out of sight. Up goes the red handkerchief – the black bitch wins!

Coursing has been a subject of controversy and protest in the recent past. There was a protest on Tuesday but, to put it in perspective, there were some ten thousand spectators and about sixty protestors. They looked rather depressed and were herded in a muddy lane with their banners by mounted police. This was probably a good thing as the Liverpuddlian crowd seemed eager to discuss things with them in a direct fashion (there had been a bomb threat to spectators earlier). I politely asked my neighbour (he of the massive arms, lager can and many-ringed ear) what he thought of the protestors? 'A load of f—g b*ll*cks, mate,' he said. Can't say fairer than that, mate, I reckon.

The Waterloo Cup is a Grand Sporting Occasion, but watch out for the Bloody Marys and do not wear your Hunt Saboteurs T-shirt.

[4]

I went to the Cheltenham Gold Cup in 1972. The crowd was so vast that you had the choice of watching the racing or getting a drink and vice versa. I swore that I would never again go racing in discomfort and retired to the depths of my armchair. But there has always been a niggling feeling that somewhere there must be a course where the occasional punter may achieve both modest comfort and a 'feast of reason and a flow of soul'. [In 1993 the opportunity presented itself.]

Kelso is a small stone town on the banks of the River Tweed. The racecourse is set in pleasant rolling countryside just to the north of the town. The old stone grandstand rears up from a clutter of pre-fab buildings which are not immediately inspiring. Mind you, a Scottish drizzle, cracked ribs and a bellyful of pain-killers do not improve the first view of anything. It took luncheon in the 'Paddock Dining Room' with its striking racing 'muriels' to start on the healing process, with excellent home-made soup and massive portions of good steak pie and chips. Then there were jolly people saying things like 'Ye'll tak anither yin in there', and 'Man, man, mak it a large yin; can ye no see the man's sair hoort'. Even at this early stage the atmosphere of Kelso began to make itself felt.

The Anglo/Scottish Borderers love good horses and are very knowledgeable; after all, in the days of the Border raids, their lives depended on choosing well. Many of the families who attend Kelso have lived, worked and fought together for generations. They feel no need for pretensions to smartness. 'Bless my soul, there's old X! He's a Racing Snob y'know: only Ascot, York, Goodwood and Cheltenham. Didn't know you bothered with Kelso, X?'

'Ah well, Weatherill's coming up, but he's lunching with Bol-linger and . . .'

'They're off!' for the first race: The Town Arms and Ladhope Inn Novices Handicap Steeple Chase. A cold wind was sweeping the course with a hint of sleety rain. Best to get bundled in amongst old sensible clothes and weather-beaten faces in the open stand and best to get a race watched before the tide of events comes sweeping along.

The rot started in the 'Doody Room', taken for the day by George Macdonald, sponsor of the first race and laird of the Town Arms in Selkirk and the Ladhope Inn in Gallowshiels. He had brought twenty-five of his first-flight customers. He had a welcoming way: 'Put anither yin in! and anither! gie the man a decent measure!' You should not drink with painkillers, they say. Ah well, the hell with it! This was Kelso and somewhere out there in the rain, The Sport of Kings Classic Racewear Novices' Hurdle was being won by Kalko. This definitely meant another dram. I was commanded to attend upon the Town Arms: 'a serious drinking place' where every night is a big night. The Ladhope is a grand place, but it seems that ladies get in there and drink Vodka and Irn Bru: George shuddered slightly.

The 'Chicken Shack' is the local name for the Directors' and Sponsors' Room. It was bursting at the seams and steam was rising from damp coats. A very brown dram was pushed into my hand by David Thomson, the Kelso Chairman. With Richard Landale (Secretary) and Johnnie Fenwick-Clennell (Clerk of the Course) he runs a tight team, whose motto is: 'Kelso must be fun'. As a result of this policy, every race is sponsored and there were 2,500 punters on a cold, wet Border Friday. I also met Reg Tweedie, the Patron, 'Mr Kelso'. Tweedie has long been a famous name in Border hunting/farming/racing. The familiar cry of 'give the man a decent dram' rang out and totally obscured the running of the Carlsberg Classic Handicap Steeple Chase. This race was won by Plenty Crack. In the Borders as many places elsewhere, 'crack' means fun and laughter. It is usually associated with whisky and has nothing to do with illicit substances.

A wander down to the parade ring seemed a good idea, but was made slow by familiar faces and firm handshakes.

'What fettle, lad?'

'Right tatty, man. I've been flat on my back for three days with the 'flu, sending the wife out to feed the tups, but it's wonderful what a bit of racing air will do, man.'

The Ship Hotel Morebattle Hurdle Race was taken in the open air for the good of the health and a feeling of being duty-bound to watch another race.

Yet another room and yet another dram; this time with the great Kenneth Oliver, the 'Benign Bishop' of northern racing. He regards Kelso as one of the top country courses in Britain: 'The course is so good that top-class trainers send top-class horses to run here and it's one of the friendliest courses in the country.' Amen to that. Hooshyerbugger! yes, a lot of water, please. A bystander points at the 'Bishop's' head: 'There's the richest reserve of racing knowledge in there and', he drops his aim, 'the richest reserve of gin in there.'

The best view of the course is from the Stewards' Control Room which is conveniently sited above the Chicken Shack and where the Stewards kindly invited me to join them for the Bollinger Rutherford Steeple Chase. The Acting Stewards for the day were Messrs C. Scott, T. G. Dunn, J. P. Elliott and Captain the Hon. G. Maitland-Carew; all very experienced men and all very jolly, Bollinger sort of people when they are off duty. Very properly they take their duties extremely seriously and soberly.

After the race, the Steward's Secretary, William Nunneley, took me to the Stewards' Room ('Where the bums get smacked'). I had always thought that Stewards' Rooms might be luxurious places with mahogany panelling and a decent glass of Port about somewhere. 'Sparse' might be a suitable description of the room at Kelso: institutional brown paint, a plain table and chairs, a charming lady typist and a mass of video equipment. Every race is recorded by three cameras: head on, side on and a remote camera out in the country. Every race can be seen frame by frame. William ran through the sequence that caused a Stewards' Enquiry to be held on the second race. The jockey's explanation had been accepted. 'If we've seen something that looks odd, the chances are that some punters will notice as well.'

It was back to the Chicken Shack for The Travail Employment

Group Cessford Hunters' Steeple Chase. There was far too much steam to see much out of the window, but there were some jolly good buttered scones to act as a little internal blotting paper.

It would have been a shameful thing to be seen to be spending the whole day drinking whisky, so it seemed meet, right and my bounden duty to visit the Bollinger chaps in their suite and drink some of their Champagne and jolly nice they and it were.

Somehow the seventh and final race (E. B. F. Peter and Gillian Allan National Hunt Novices' Hurdle Race – Qualifier) must have slipped by me without being noticed. It is possible that I may have been tied up in the Directors' Bar. There was a large young man who found broken ribs very funny and was trying to make me laugh and I was explaining that I had not laughed since 1972 and he tried to prod me in the ribs with his cigar and his wife came and led him away by the ear and then I did laugh. So that is Kelso: good racing, nice people, grand atmosphere and Plenty Crack.

[5]

'Go,' they said, 'and wrestle with the ladies.' They were sniggering.

The Third European Amateur Arm Wrestling Championship took place in Britain this year [1993] at the Queen's Hotel, Crystal Palace, under the control of the British Arm Wrestling Federation. Those who have never heard of the BAWF (and I must number myself amongst them) should be properly ashamed of themselves. The Federation was formed eleven years ago and now has nearly 4,000 members in the UK and is seeking Sports Council recognition. I learned all this from Kim Shoesmith, the Federation Secretary, who did not look at all muscle-bound and was fighting bravely against food poisoning.

In case you are not familiar with Arm Wrestling, two opponents face each other across a table; with elbows firmly planted, they clasp their right hands; at the signal they each try to force the other's hand down until it touches the table. It is as simple, or as complicated, as that.

The entrance steps to the hotel were blocked by a seething polyglot mass of brightly coloured shell suits: sixteen nations were trying to sort out their group photographs in a babel of mutual incomprehension. There being, as yet, no EC directive on good manners, the only way in was by direct assault with a briefcase: '*Excusez moi!*' I cried. 'Me Rowssian' came the unenthusiastic response.

The event was happening in a rather sinister basement suite. Here I met Katherine Monbint, a most attractive lady who is currently British Women's 70 kgs Champion. There are twelve different weight categories for men and seven for women and it is not my fault if that is sexist. Katherine started wrestling at school. She is an Alternative Therapist, runs a video production company, trains six days a week and has so far 'escaped marriage': she would hardly have the time. She runs a lot. Is that important? You have to develop the top of the body for Arm Wrestling and you want the bottom bit to stay in proportion, do you not?

The hall was filling quickly now. They are a cheerful, noisy crowd the Arm Wrestlers, their clothing multi-hued as macaws and embroidered with slogans in many languages: 'Federation Bras de Fer' (Belgium); 'Lucha de Brazos' (Spain). The Scots are more personalised: 'Granite Arm', 'The Hand', 'Big J'.

A blast of martial music greeted the appearance of Chairman Ray Power who announced that Ray Ballard from the Isle of Sheppey was going to sing an anthem, composed especially for the occasion, called 'The Arm Wrestling Song' to a tune that everybody would recognise. I did not. It seems that it is a tune called 'Get Ready' and is no doubt 'high in the charts' or something. Unfortunately the decibel level was so high that both the tune and the words got lost, but I am sure that we all gave Mr Ballard full marks for his plucky attempt at Presley Pelvic Pumping; it certainly got the audience going.

There was no 'race card' available, I suppose on the basis that everybody knew who everybody was anyway. The competitors were only known by their country and a number, as it might be: 'France 86'. This led to confusion as the numbers were only announced in English and a lot of competitors had no English. The roll call of competitors did take rather a long time, but led to some interesting line ups on the stage of assorted shapes, sizes and hairstyles. Each competitor received a rapturous welcome from the national supporters. 'Granite Arm' was bellowing something that could only be construed as: 'Doon yer airse, Bobby!'

Two bouts at a time took place on the stage. An average bout takes about six seconds. It has to be said that, to the uninitiated, the visual impact is minimal. Mr X (he had skipped work), who had come all the way from Farnham out of 'sheer curiosity', said that I looked knowledgeable and could I explain the finer points to him? He picked a bummer there.

Things hotted up with a bout between a tiny Israeli and a diminutive Belgian who would have to be described as a 'Central African Person of Restricted Growth' and who had not quite grasped the sporting nature of the contest. He came to the table stamping and roaring. He then came a right moody with the Ref for making him change his grip and roared some more. The Ref waved him off the stage. The Belgian did a war dance, roaring the while. Three large Belgians eventually picked him up bodily and bore him from the room, still roaring.

There was an interesting contest between one of our brave lads and a German. Forearm to forearm they strained and twisted, faces contorted, legs entwined round table legs. 'Granite Arm' was bellowing: 'Feel him out, Nige; feel him out!' I was beginning to have doubts about 'Granite Arm'. Nige eventually wiped out the Kr—, sorry, German and they went into a deep cuddle.

The atmosphere was warming up into a fine gymnasium fug, helped by incessant 'Rock' muzak and moderate air conditioning. It was time for a Vodka and Tonic. 'No alcohol, mate,' said the man leaning on the bar, 'it inflames the foreigners' and some of them were quite flammable already. I had just heard a French man bellowing to a winsome French elf that she should '*arrache le bras*', which I translate as 'Tear her arm off'. There had also been a blast of Spanish which contained the word '*puta*', which is definitely not for *Telegraph* readers.

There were more women's bouts now which also raised the temperature. The ladies really put their all into it and their passions lie close to the surface; very close in the case of Italian ladies and even closer in the case of an ash blonde, plaited Brunhilda from Finland who had a real wobbly. The photographic student who was investigating 'the effect of sport on human behaviour' should have had something to chew on.

Nige was back in action, with support from 'Granite Arm'. 'No prisoners, Nige! Take him out!'

They would not let me wrestle a lady, they said, me being 19 stone and all, but eventually a nice lady called Kim Holman (up and coming in the 70 kgs) agreed to sacrifice herself.

Elbows on the table, her tiny hand in mind, take the strain, muscles bulging, this was unfair, I was going to massacre the poor girl, still think of 'Granite Arm': no prisoners, eh Jummy?

Kim flattened me with ease; twice. Well, I mean, I was not ready and she was trained and . . . No, she was better and my thanks to her. My thanks also to all the Arm Wrestlers: they are a lovely cheerful bunch of people and I wish them well.

As I left, Brunhilda was sitting on the steps, scowling like a troll. I was quite pleased that she had not got hold of my arm, or something; that would have been the absolute finish.

12. WINTER

[1]

'The Opening Meet' – now there is an evocative phrase for a countryman. It is usually held on the first Saturday in November.

We have our opening meet at Pennymuir. It is a bleak crossroads high in the Border hills – and I mean 'bleak'. Even in high summer the weather at Pennymuir can be dour and dreich. This made the weather of the opening meet even more amazing. It was a day of windless sunshine after a frosty night. The air was clear and cold and seared the lungs. It was what the Cornish call 'a day lent' – on the basis that it will have to be repaid with interest at some time in the future.

There was a tremendous scene of cars and horse boxes at the meet, with visitors from far and near. There were hands to be shaken and ladies to be kissed and that wonderful phrase that I love to hear – 'Ye'll tak a dram noo, Wullie?' The answer to this one is – 'Yes, please!' (not wishing to give offence by refusing, you understand). In fact, whilst I was still refusing to give offence, hounds had moved off and had found in the bog below the meet. There was a great burst of cry from the hounds. Now all was frantic bustle – tightening of girths, heaving into saddles ('Oh, do stand still, you bloody horse!'), revving of motor bikes – make haste! make haste! for hounds were running and me with my quadricycle still on the trailer.

Hounds did a big circle out on the hill and then came roaring back into the covert by the meet – which put me nicely at the front.

Hounds hunt foxes entirely by scent. Bright sunny days are not normally good conditions, but that day was an exception – hounds were flying. They flew away from the covert and out over the open hill behind the meet with seventy-odd horses and thirty assorted bikes in hot pursuit. I went in the opposite direction. 'Old dogs for hard roads' the saying goes. After nigh on fifty years of hunting, this old dog has learned something about hunted foxes. A run fox seldom goes straight. He tends to run in an arc and, once you have worked out the angle of the arc, you can bisect it. It works – sometimes. It worked this time. With Craig perched on the back pannier, we chugged down to the bridge – 'Yonder they go!' Craig (14) has the sharpest eyes in the business. Hounds were flying like a flock of gulls across the great sweeping hillside in front of us. The rest of the bikes and the horses were a parish behind. There was no time to delay. Hounds were already disappearing over the top of Humblemoor.

The view from the hill top was magical. In the clear frosty air, you could see the blue line of the Lammermuirs, far to the north. To the south, fold upon fold of hills rolled away to the distant bulk of the great Cheviot itself. But there was little time for views.

Hounds were already on the opposite hill, a mile away across the steep valley, and it was bump, grind and bounce – 'Hooshyer-bugger! we nearly cowped there!' – down to the track in the bottom. Another bisection of the angle and we were up beside the next rocky burn in time to see hounds streaming across and Craig pointing to the lithe red fox slipping easily across a scree face half a mile in front.

It was past 2 pm when we looked across another gulch and saw hounds disappearing into the forestry on Swindon Hill – not many followers left now.

'Not worth going *there*, there'll be foxes all ways,' said one. 'They'll be there for the night.' But with hunting, you never know. Never mind where the others were going – down through the farm for us and along the track to the next valley – after all, you never know. Sure enough, there was a party of hounds running like stoor (dust) on the opposite face. The hunt was on and only five of us on bikes and quads left in it – we'd best be sharp or we'd lose them. On, on, bouncing and clattering through rock, heather and bull snouts, deep into the territory of the neighbouring hunt – this was not just a hunt now, it was a border raid. In the failing light we saw hounds disappear into another block of forestry, and that was that for us.

What an opening meet. The trip switch on the quad showed that we had covered some forty miles of wild hill country – the Dear knows what distance hounds covered. It was as Craig (a chap of few words) said, 'A very canny day.'

[2]

There are Opening Meets like the one described above, and there are Opening Meets where everything conspires against you, particularly the weather.

★   ★   ★

It was thick fog. Ah well, I thought, it might be better over the Border, which is where the opening meet was. But it was not. I crawled all the way to the meet with headlights on and all the time the fret kept crawling in from the North Sea on a south-east wind – nothing good ever comes out of that airt.

At the meet, the clustered lorries and cars loomed out of the mist. There was an excited chorus from the hound van and the occasional impatient stamp from a horse box, but the fact was that nobody was going anywhere in a hurry – except into the village hall for a restoring glass or two.

Hunting is entirely at the mercy of the weather and, as we know, the weather controls the scenting conditions, and hounds hunt a fox by its scent. As a sort of rough guide, scent lies when the glass is rising (ah! thank you, Jim, you took the hint – just a small one) or steady (just a drop of water, please) but when the barometer is falling then the scent rises. If *you* can smell a fox then the scent is not down where hounds need it. Certain weather conditions can stop hunting. Deep snow stops it because it is impossible to get about. Hard frost can be a problem: hounds can cut the pads of their feet on frozen ground and horses are certainly not designed for skating. Wind can knacker the job and the winds on the Cheviots can extract wisdom teeth. As another rough guide – if the wind is so strong that you cannot open a gate against it, then it is best to stay at home.

In some ways, fog is the worst of all because it is difficult to make a clear decision. The fog may lift. It is demoralising to decide not to hunt only for the fog to lift when you are halfway home. So it tends to be a case of 'giving it another half hour' and wandering about telling each other that it is 'hellish, altogether' and that 'it is definitely lifting. I can see the end of the field' – until someone points out that the village hall has now vanished behind you. At least there is compensation if the meet is at a pub (especially for the landlord). There was the occasion when glances at the bar window kept confirming the thickness of the fog. It was not until 12.30 that someone thought to wipe the window pane – to find brilliant sunshine outside. This was not to be for us that day. For an hour we sat in the soggy, clinging dampness. I thought it hopeless, but our master is made of stern stuff and a banging of tailboards, a stamping of horses and excited hound voices indicated a departure. By the time that I had got my quad off the trailer, hounds, horses and followers had disappeared in the murk.

It was fortunate that scent was poor and that hounds did not go anywhere very much nor very fast. We could hear them, but we only got occasional glimpses of them, looming momentarily out of the wrack, before disappearing again as the grey vapour rolled relentlessly past us. Anyone who knows hills will know how disorientated you can become in fog, even on ground you know well. I got lost out on the hill. Then I found a tractor track that eventually took me down below the cloud, but also somewhere quite different to where I thought I ought to be.

No one complained when the Master decided to pack up rather earlier than usual. We were all rather glad to get back to the meet at about 4 pm and, as we did, the fog cleared – *c'est la chasse.*

[3]

There is a lot of loose talk about the Beatles (a group of itinerant musicians, one understands) and the Swingin' Sixties.

So, how swung the Sixties for me? The answer is – very little. I never had a pair of flares nor a caftan. When I wore a suit it was one that I had inherited from my grandfather. The nearest thing to a hallucinogen that passed my lips was the cider they made at the Union Inn – believe me, you found some funny things in it and saw some funny things after it. The Union cider also had some very real and pressing after-effects – as old Ernest used to say: 'You always want to have a wisp of hay in your pocket, when you'm walking home from the Union.' Anyone who is furrowing their brow over this reference has never experienced the brutally cathartic qualities of rough cider – does you a power of good.

What else did I not do in the Sixties? Ah yes – I did not have long hair, for the very good reason that long hair looks ghastly under a hunting cap and I was a stickler for correct turn-out. This is why 'Peter the Boy' was such a problem. A little background here, I think. In 1964, I become the youngest and, almost certainly, the stupidest Master of Foxhounds in the country. I 'did' for myself and lived in great squalor and a tiny cottage at the kennels. From there I went forth with my hounds three days of the week to hunt the wild foxes on the even wilder hills of Dartmoor.

The economists amongst you may like to reflect on the fact that the hunt gave me an annual allowance of £2,000 out of which it was expected that all the expenses of kennel and stable would be paid, the motor vehicles run and maintained, the wages of a full-time man and a girl groom in the winter be found. I allowed myself the princely sum of £5 per week (the agricultural wage was c.£8, I think). This £5 a week then would keep me fed (just about) and cidered, but there was no margin for swinging – even had I been so inclined. Anyway, I was much too busy worrying about Peter the Boy.

The Missus was an amazing lady who had hunted the Dartmoor hounds herself for some fourteen seasons. She came to my rescue when inexperience threatened to sink me. She took over the running of the stables. She stammered, had a Corporal Major's command of invective and hated girl grooms ('They're either in my bbbloody way, or the ffffamily way'). Then she said – 'Found you a tttopping bbboy; right off the bbback of the mmmoor; rough as a bbbadger's arse.' This was Peter. He was a good boy (if rather dreamy) except for his flowing shoulder-length golden locks – wouldn't go with a hunting cap, d'yersee. I tried all ways to get him to cut his hair, all to no avail. 'Dddon't worry,' said the Missus, 'I'll see to it,' but the Opening Meet (maximum smartness) got nearer and Peter's hair got longer.

The day before the opening meet, the Missus was clipping the horses, with Peter holding the headcollars and dreaming. I looked into the stables. The clipping was finished. The Missus was by the wooden chair that she used to stand on to reach the higher bits of horse, oiling the electric clippers. 'Ah!' said she to me, 'you're just in time. Now, Peter, I think the Master told you to gget your hair cut and I told him that I would help!' – at this she seized a fist full of golden locks and pushed the yelling boy down onto the wooden chair – 'Now you bbbugger! bide still or I'll cut your fff—g ear off!' All round the head buzzed the clippers. Down fell the golden tresses, until there was just a little top knot left: 'There now,' said the Missus, studying her handiwork, 'tttold you I'd ggget his hair cut.' Ah yes, they were good old days, the Sixties.

[4]

St Hubert is the patron saint of Hunting and his day is 3 November – the opening of the French hunting season.

There are over 300 official hunts in France with a variety of quarries – red deer, roe deer, hare, fox, rabbit, boar. There are now only two hunts with the *sanglier* (wild boar) as their sole quarry. One of these is the Rallye Chapeau.

The Rallye Chapeau hangs its collective hat in the Bourbonnais which is near as dammit the extreme centre of France. This is *France profonde* – a pretty rolling country of grass fields with their white Charollais cattle and great oak woods, where the secretive wild pigs live. They come out at night to feast on the maize fields of the peasant (a very respectable description in France) farmers. The peasants only like pig on a plate.

As regular readers will know, the Memsahib and I have been going to the Rallye Chapeau every year for six years. A recent invitation from the Comtesse Henri de Monspey (whose hounds they are) et des Membres de l'Equipage to attend the Mass of Saint-Hubert was not one to refuse. We stayed at the Château de Vieux Chambord where the Devaulx de Chambord family have lived since 12-something.

It is no good going hunting unless you know where the pigs are. *Sanglier* are nocturnal and peripatetic. They can be lying in wood A one day and twelve miles away in wood B the next. So you have to *faire le bois* – the wood in question being La Goute de Cerf, some 4,000 hectares of oak woodland. At 0715 Thibault (the son of the house) and I set out for a rendezvous at an isolated farm. There were a dozen people in the kitchen drinking coffee 'with'. Each person is allocated a section of forest and an experienced hound (*chien du bois*) on a lead. He then tramps round his section looking for traces of pig and hoping that the hound will '*faire le connaissance*' – wind the pigs in the thickets. We were issued with Foudras – a lanky Blanc et Noir (a breed of French hound). For an hour we tramped the muddy rides through stands of oak and beech. Thibault was searching the ground all the time for footprints, but it had been a wet night and pigs tend to stay in bed when it rains. However, as we passed a thicket, Foudras suddenly came alert, straining at his lead and whining – there were pigs about.

Back at the château there was only time for a quick cup of coffee and it was off to the meet. We must not be *en retard* for the Messe, although in France nothing actually happens on time because everybody is too busy talking. The Messe was held in a marquee in the grounds of the Château de Fougis, the home of M. Clayeux. The temporary altar was decorated with flowers, bracken, hunting horns and a mounted boar's head.

People came thick and fast and from far and near, the *chasseurs* wearing boots like the Household Cavalry, the long-skirted coats in the colours of their hunts and the curling French hunting horns. In Britain only the huntsman carries a horn. In France many hunt members carry them. They are a vital part of the proceedings. There are some 300 tunes (fanfares). Every part of a hunt has a fanfare (even down to crossing a railway). This means that you can stand in a forest and know just what is happening, sight unseen, by listening to the horns. Every hunt has its own ceremonial fanfares, as does every Master.

Fanfares announced M. L'Abbé Lepée, the Priest of Jaligny, a jolly-looking chap. The marquee was full, with many people standing outside. It was a beautiful Mass with a large choir conducted by Mme Devaulx de Chambord. The abbé, an ardent fisherman, gave a very funny sermon, the gist of which was that hunting and the Church were good because they bring people together. After the Mass everybody moved outside for the blessing. There must have been 500 people. The hounds were brought round onto the lawn and were ceremoniously blessed by the priest: 'Whatever anybody else says, the Good Lord approves of hunting' – Amen. There was general consent that it was one of the best St Hubert's Masses for many years.

There was a pause for refreshment – a serious business in France. Then the Men of the Wood lined up in front of the Comtesse and gave their *rapports* – 'Madame, I have the honour to report . . .' The Master then decided to which part of the forest the hounds would be taken.

I do not ride any more, so we (and a considerable luncheon basket) were driven by Mme de Chambord – hereinafter referred to as Mme. Mme drives French-fast with great skill and scares the tripes out of me. We drove to the outside of the forest and waited. Nothing much was happening. There were occasional distant fanfares; a buzzard mewing overhead; ham, sausage, pâté and cheese to be eaten and other car followers appearing waving bottles of wine. It was a lovely day. A sudden hard-driven car (I estimate there were at least 200 cars) – a scatter of urgent French – three pigs found – two had left the forest – hounds were on – *Mon Dieu! vite! vite!* – bottles, glasses, bread into the back and Mme was away whilst my feet were still hanging out of the door. I would have to sharpen up.

I have compared car-following a hunt in France to blitzkreig × rally cross. We kept meeting other hunting cars going in the opposite direction – much shouting, gesticulating and conflicting intelligence. We would hear an occasional distant fanfare. Mme made a bold forward cast, but just too far. We whizzed back to find a jam of cars and horses. The boar (a young pig of about 100 livres – hunting is not metricated) had been taken and we had missed it – *merde!* We had not even seen a boar yet – despondency.

But what was this? Another fluttered messenger in a van and a hurry – eight hounds with another boar (*'un gros'*) on the other side of the forest – *vite! vite!* Villy, *vite!* vroom! vroom! We found a heap of excited cars and some fanfaring. The boar had just crossed the road in the forest – we had just missed him. More *vitesse* to the outside of the forest – we listened, but it was difficult to hear for furious French persons telling each other to be quiet. A distant fanfare – *'C'est Tobie* [the Master's son] *il a sonné la Changement du Forêt'* – this fanfare means that the boar has gone to a different wood. Mount! mount! mount! *en voiture! en voiture!*

The other wood – a gesticulation of cars – the boar (*'vraiment un gros'*) had just crossed the road – out came the *trompes* (horns) – fanfare, *'Sanglier avant'*, then *'Bien aller'*. There came the bold eight hounds who had stuck to the line so well. A storm of holloaing on the road cheered them on – 'La! La! La! Ho! Ho! Ho!' – and roaring up the road came the hound van with the hounds from the other hunt – 'La! La!'

'Vite! Villy! *Vite!'* to another part of the wood – all the hounds were on together now and the cry was tremendous in the forest. Amongst the woods was a field and a lake and suddenly there he was, a great black shape, but moving with surprising agility, but hounds were hard at him now and he took to the lake (*sonnez le Bat l'Eau*), out the other side and stood at bay (*L'hallali par terre*) in the trees and was despatched. He was indeed a big boar.

Le fin you might think – all go home – not in France. The boar has to be properly honoured at the Curée – an obligatory ceremony that takes place, come rain, come snow and by headlights if necessary. The boar was skinned and the choice bits removed to be distributed to local farmers. The skin was replaced on the remains. The *chasseurs* formed up and the story of the day was told in fanfares. Then the skin was whipped off and the hounds who had been waiting with mounting impatience got their reward. Then, more fanfares – those of the Masters and any visiting dignitaries and then the farewell.

Le fin, now? oh no, not in France – always there is a *diner* and a post mortem of the day that rushes remorselessly and in spate through many courses and bottles.

The Rallye Chapeau gave old Saint Hubert a great day – I hope that he was proud of them.

[5]

I sat in the sunshine amongst the frost-rimed heather and watched the fox. He had been hunted for a bit earlier on. Hounds had hit off his drag (the scent line from his early morning peregrinations) and had worked it out painstakingly along the frozen hillside, down across the tumbling burn and up to the deep heather on the sheltered side of Ravens Cleugh where he had lain up for the day. There they 'put him off'.

A fox relies on scent for filling his belly and so he knows when scenting conditions are good or bad. He had been in no great hurry as he took hounds across the valley below the steading then over the hill on the other side. It was here that a fresh fox must have jumped up in front of hounds and they, rejoicing in the much stronger scent, had gone up and away, best pace, to the Scottish Border and beyond.

For perhaps half an hour I watched the original 'run' fox. He was dawdling. The thing that keeps a fox moving on is noise – as long as he can hear hounds behind him, he keeps moving. Hounds were away out of hearing. The fox had come trotting over the hill. He stopped and listened and slowed to a walk. He was following a sheep trod. He stopped and had a good scratch. Then he found an interesting smell and followed it round the tumble of stones in a syke (small declivity). It came to nothing, so he sat in the gathering warmth of the sun for a bit. Then he had another scratch and ambled on across some bare ground before he disappeared from view in a patch of dead bracken. I wished him good luck and went to Scotland to see what hounds were doing.

[6]

I have before me a battered little red booklet called *The Fox's Prophecy*. This copy was published in 1918. The original is thought to have been written by a Mr D. W. Nash c. 1870. This was a time of the Franco/Prussian war which resulted in a crushing defeat for the French. Mr Nash was full of forebodings for the future with the emergence of a triumphant and ambitious military power in the middle of Europe. In the 1918 edition, the foreword by Thomas Kingscote suggests that Mr Nash's forebodings were justified and that the events of 1870 gave rise to the 1914–18 war. However, the prophecy has much that is worthy of thought in 1994 and deserves reading.

So what is this prophecy? It is a poem. Tom Hill was huntsman to the Cotswold Hounds in the 1860s. In the poem, Hill is in tatty fettle because he has lost his hounds: 'He thought, I must essay to find / my hounds at any cost / A huntsman who has lost his hounds / is but a huntsman lost.' Then he sees an old fox 'grim and gaunt of limb' whose eye 'shone with an unearthly fire'. As this is an unearthly fox it is not surprising that it speaks English: 'Last of my race, to me 'tis given / the future to unfold'. The old fox is gloomy about the future: 'Too well I know, by wisdom taught / the existence of my race / o'er all wide England's green domain / is bound up with the Chase. Better in early youth and strength / the race for life to run / than poisoned like the noxious rat / or slain by felon gun'. Well, yes, maybe, you may say, he would be made to say that, would he not? but listen on a bit: 'The woodlands where my race has bred / unto the axe shall yield / hedgerow and copse shall cease to shade / the ever-widening field. The furzy down, the moorland heath / the steam plough shall invade / Nor park nor manor shall escape / common, nor forest glade'.

Now I suspect that more contemporary interest may be aroused, but you ain't heard nothing yet. Now the old fox really lets rip: 'Time-honoured creeds and ancient faith / the Altar and the Crown / Lordship's hereditary right / before the tide go down.'

He suggests that 'religion shall be held a jest / and loyalty a crime'. And how about this for a prophetic utterance: 'The homes where love and peace shall dwell / fierce politics shall vex / and unsexed woman strive to prove / herself the coarser sex'. Does that not ring the bell of truth? as does: 'Honour and truth – old-fashioned words / the noisy mob deride'.

The old fox was into defence cuts too: 'Her army and her navy / Britain shall cast aside / Soldiers and ships are costly things / defence an empty pride'. The fox was even prescient of the EC: 'Disarmed before the foreigner / the knee shall humbly bend / and yield the treasures that she lacked / the wisdom to defend'. There is more, much more that is stunningly applicable to Little Britain in 1994. What a pity our own dear Prime Minister has never found the time to put Trollope aside for a minute and read *The Fox's Prophecy*. He would find himself and all the rest of the Westminster Gang neatly encapsulated therein and much of what that old fox foretold in 1871 has come to pass. It remains to say that the Prophecy has a happy ending. We can only hope that the prophecy is as correct about the years to come as it has been uncannily accurate about the recent past.

Read it for yourself, if you get the chance. The little book has been many years out of print, but not out of truth.

NOTE: I later used this poem as the basis of a little book, retaining the title *The Fox's Prophecy*. I wrote a 1990's commentary to it and Diana Brown (*see* page 136) provided some wonderful illustrations for it.

[7]

You will be reading this on my birthday; a good moment to remember my Birthday Hunt.

This all happened a long, long time ago. It was a still raw

morning with a dirty lowering sky. The black shaggy Galloway cattle had come down to the moor edge from the high tops. It was going to snow. You could smell it. All hunting depends on following the scent of the hunted animal. The only certainty about scent is that it is uncertain. One of the few times that you can bet on a good scent is before snow.

Hounds were quickly speaking in a snug patch of whins on the west side of Spittalcombe. The cry was tremendous, but it was obvious that the pack had split. As Jim's holloa announced the departure of a fox from the top of the whins, a big old stager poked out at the bottom and was off like a sailor on a run ashore. I could see the other hounds streaming out over the crag, but mine were already tumbling across the rocky river in the bottom. It was time to ram the hat down and ride. As we skidded, skated and hopped down the boulder-strewn slope, I thanked the Lord that I was on Red Knight, my best moor horse; he of the six legs and as many gears.

In my memory, I can still ride every step of that hunt and many steps we had of it, right out, straight out, for the top of the moor and the 'stuggy'. This is a huge sponge where the rivers rise; it can only be crossed with care and then only in certain places. We were only getting distant glimpses of the flying hounds, but their cry came back loud and clear. We were approaching the Black Mire when the first snowflake hit my nose. There is a track across the Black Mire, but it is not always easy to see, even in good weather. In places it is only a couple of feet wide and actually goes up and down as you cross it. There is no margin for error, for the Mire will swallow a horse. I should have turned back, as did the remnant of the followers, and I think that I would have turned back had I been on any other horse. We went on. The snow was settling in now. Visibility was down to a few yards and how I thanked the Lord when the old horse and I crept out on the other side of that ghastly place. Hounds had disappeared completely and we were alone in a white world. The only thing was to jog on and remember that every stream runs into a river and every river runs into the sea. My stream eventually brought me to a stone wall, a gate and huge relief. I had been very foolish and the moor does not suffer fools. The gate gave me a rough track which led downhill to civilisation or its outpost, the lonely farm of High Brimicombe. There was no longer any question of trying to find hounds; just self-preservation.

As we sank down the long valley, the snow turned to sleet and then bitter, chilling rain. It was nearly dark, but light enough to see a figure coming up the track. It was old Grafter, a senior doghound; he was heading for his distant kennel, now some fifteen miles away. He was carrying a fox's brush in his mouth. I leapt off and hugged the old dog. He gave me the brush and licked my face. Our little party set off downhill.

The lights of Low Brimicombe were a beacon of hope and what a wonderful sight to see the hound van parked in the yard and full of hounds. I blew my horn and out of the house came Jim and Farmer Jan. With Grafter safely tucked in with his mates and Red Knight in the stable being wisped down by Jan Jr, it was into the warm kitchen for tea and whisky and an excited account of how hounds had caught their fox against the wall of the shippen (cowshed) and how Jan had rung the kennels just before Jim had also rung in to see if there was any news of me. Jan said that he had tried to get the brush, but a 'gert big old bugger' had gone off with it. And Jim? his lot had also had a tremendous run and, with a flourish, he pulled a brush from his pocket, just as I did the same. 'Well, I'm buggered,' said Jan, 'in't that a proper job.' He filled my glass. ''Appy Birthday, My 'Andsome!' and so it was.

[8]

Do not think that you can just barge in and be Santa Claus (a.k.a. Father Christmas). Ho! Ho! Ho! Ho! No, mate. You have got to work your way up; learn the trade; start by making the tea and sweeping the floor. I mean, you would not believe the mess them Elves make, knocking out all them toys, and as for the Reindeer – well, you just don't want to know, take it from me.

Day 1:
So how do you start? In my case I went to the Gateshead Metro Centre, Europe's largest shopping centre; a wonderland of shops and restaurants, squeakily clean and hermetically sealed from wind, weather and dreary everyday reality – except when it comes to getting your thrifty (purse) out. At the Administrative Offices I stood, shuffling my worn boots and twisting my cap in my gnarled hands under the piercing collective gaze of Karen, the Marketing Manager, and Paul from PR.

'I suppose that he could start as an Elf,' said Karen.

'He's not very elf-like,' said Paul doubtfully, eyeing my 18 stone bulk. I was with him all the way; I mean, you hear things about elves, don't you? like them having certain 'proclivities' and all. No, definitely not an Elf. 'Well, I suppose he could be a Gnome then.' Now, that was more like it; good, solid, brawny chaps Gnomes and so that was it: I was enrolled as the first ever (wait for it) METRO GNOME.

There are two Santas at the Metro Centre – John and Cyril. My initiation was to be under the firm, but gentle, tutelage of Cyril who was working the afternoon shift. But first I had to find Santa's Grotto and if you want to produce some interesting reactions from the Great British Public, then try walking about in a multi-hued tunic and a cap with bells on it, carrying a Mr Punch tickling stick.

Santa's Grotto was located at 'Town Square No. 1', one of the many open spaces that punctuate the Metro Centre. Here a little Victorian village had been built complete with carol singers, hurdy-gurdy men, chestnut roasters and skaters, all in perpetual mechanical motion. The little gate that let you into the village was snecked. A sign said: 'Closed – Santa has gone to feed the Reindeer'. In fact, Santa was sitting in his grotto in relaxed mode with his wig and beard off and in the company of the lovely Sara and Beverley who were dressed in very fetching crinolines. Who were they? Santa's helpers of course, and very nice too. There was no sign of the reindeer in the Grotto, but a strong smell of Salt 'n' Vinegar Crisps.

Santa Cyril is a lovely gentle man to whom santa-clausing is a very important and serious business. He was doubtful about the Press, having just been sent up in a local paper. But the business was afoot. It was time for the helpers to don their fur-trimmed bonnets and open the gate and for Santa and his Gnome to close up for action.

The action was relentless. The queue had been formed for an hour and so it was hardly surprising that some of the parents looked more than a little worn round the edges. To queue for an hour with an eager and impatient child, and that in the middle of Christmas shopping, is likely to fray people a bit. Mr Punch and I did our best to cheer them up, but I have to say that we had more success with the children (well, some children) than we did with the adults. I got the feeling that some of them would have liked to have done something anatomically difficult to Mr Punch and to me. I suppose that to queue for an hour and then to be confronted by an 18-stone Gnome, tinkling his bells at you, might just drive a man to drink.

But, like all great actors, we persevered. Mr Punch did a wonderful job (apart from the occasional child who burst into tears at the sight of him). He very kindly invited children to punch him on his beaky nose, whereupon he emitted a most satisfactory noise and cried, 'That's the way to do it!!' Anyone who thinks children are not naturally prone to violence should have seen the alacrity with which the little dears went for the neb and there was the little boy who repeatedly head-butted poor Mr Punch: I am sure that he will go far in Gateshead society.

Of course, you always get the spoilsports, like the little know-all who cried: 'Mam! Mam! It's not Mr Punch speaking; it's that Gnome. I can see his lips moving!'

'Oh no, you can't!'

'I can, I can. It's *you*, it's not Mr Punch, is it, Mam? Mam?'

Mam raised her eyes to Heaven, no doubt seeking the Divine guidance that she must have so needed in her life with a child monster.

All through the long hours, my respect for Cyril increased. He was kind and gentle and the children responded to him. Each one sat on Santa's Treasure Chest and told him about their presents and hopes. Cyril's patience was boundless. He was everything that a child thinks Santa Claus ought to be, although how he and I are going to get all those bicycles down the chimneys I really do not know.

Day 2:
The moment of truth: I was deemed qualified to be Santa.

I arrived at the Metro Centre with a specially hired Santa Suit because your average Santa is, well, average size. Was I nervous? who would not be nervous of such a heavy responsibility and that is what it is. No one who has seen the rapt faces and the wonderment of little bairns meeting Santa can doubt that. The man who would be Santa holds a lot of hope and dreams. Some cannot take it. The Metro Centre had an unhappy experience a few years ago: a Santa full of the wrong kind of Christmas spirit and blotto in his grotto.

When I arrived at the Grotto the queue wound down the 'village' street and Cyril was hard at it. I was still in my civvies. The sight of two Santas might just twist a young mind.

'Ah ha! here comes the Plumber! Have you come to mend the reindeers' trough, Mr Plumber?'

'That's right, Santa; I'll have it done in 4 ho-hos,' and with my carrier bag, I slipped into the tiny dressing-room beside the throne and pulled the curtain. Strip down to the underpants, because the grotto is hotto, and on with the red trousers; on with the 'fur'-trimmed red tunic; into the welly boots (from which I had scoured the mud and sheep muck that morning) then the wig and the beard and the hat; a deep breath and:

'I've fixed, it, Santa.'

'Right, Mr Plumber.' The Grotto was sealed off for a moment

for the change. I looked 'about right' and Cyril disappeared behind the curtain. I was on: Ho! Ho! Ho! By the way Cyril says that English Santas do not say 'Ho! Ho! Ho!' It is an American idea, he says, but I cannot resist breaking out on occasion.

So there I was; on the throne. Sara opened the grotto door. A little face peeped round the corner and immediately burst into tears and buried its face against Mum. Not all the combined cajoling and soothing of Mum, Nan and Auntie could persuade the child (sex never determined) to face this terrible old man in a long white beard. It was a fine start. A whisper from behind the curtain told me not to worry, it happens. It got better. The thing that got to me was the sheer wonder on most of the little faces: some were shy, some impassive, some happy, some matter of fact, but the realisation quickly came that they all *believed* absolutely; to them *I was Santa* and if I mucked it up, then I was going to ruin a child's Christmas. No one wants that. I went for it.

It was a fairly simple routine and you need a routine if you are going to survive several hours. I was doing it for an afternoon, but John and Cyril keep it up for a five- to six-hour shift, six days a week for six weeks. That is quite an act and you need a routine:

'Hallo! Have you come to see Santa? Are you going to come and sit on my box? (This is a little wickerwork chest that sits beside the throne. Kids no longer get to sit on Santa's knee – the child abuse industry has knocked that one on the head.) What's your name? oh, that's a nice name and how old are you? really; you're a big lad/lass for your age, aren't you? Now, are you going to tell Santa what you want for Christmas? a bike? everybody wants a bike this year. I hope I shall have enough to go round. But don't worry, I'll make sure that the elves (lazy little beggars) make one specially for you and put it on the sleigh. Now, have you got a chimney? do you think that Santa will be able to get the bike down the chimney? do you think that Santa will be able to get down the chimney? You don't know? What does Mum/Dad/Nan think? oh, that's all right then. And listen, you've got to promise to be asleep, I can't come in if you are awake. And you have got to promise to be *very* good between now and Christmas

192

because Santa only visits *good* children. And, to help you be good, here's a game to play. Whose picture is that? is that me? that's right, it *is* me, Santa Claus, and look, there's Frosty the Snowman. Now, if you just stand up. Do you know what you have been sitting on? It's Santa's Treasure Chest!! (open chest) and you can choose a pencil (glittery) or a little Santa! There now! off you go then and *merry Christmas* (enthusiastic waving), *merry Christmas, pet*!!

And so it went. Cyril had been whispering encouragement through the curtain whilst he changed, then:

'I've fixed the leak, Santa.'

'Thank you, Mr Plumber,' and away went Cyril. I was on my own.

And still they came: child after child: dark children, fair children, fat children; children with dummies firmly rammed in mouth; children smeared with ice cream and chocolate; children clinging to Teddy for comfort, children . . . just children.

Then there were the parents: parents of every size and shape and temperament ('Please, Santa, tell him he's got to sleep in his own bed'). Some were determined that little Craig, or Sharon, were going to sparkle to Santa even if it killed them; I think that Santa might be putting some itching powder in those parents' knickers when he drops in on Christmas Eve.

Then there was my three year-old-niece who announced loudly that 'that's not Santa, that's Anty (sic) Willy'; the little sneak.

Then there was the heavy mob of farmers' wives, come to extract the Michael, who announced that they had queued for an hour to be kissed by Santa.

Then there was Santa John, heavily disguised as the Plumber come to mend that dratted trough again (I mean, the reindeer were nearly up to their hocks in water) and my stint was over.

That is the end of the story, except that there is no end to the Santa story and if you want him to visit *you* on Christmas Eve, then you must be very good and sleep in your own bed.

★

[9]

It is New Year's Day. It is snowing. I have got influenza. It is a good moment to think about Hypocrisy.

I hunt for 'fur and feather' and make no secret about the fact that I enjoy it. My attitudes often conflict with those who might be called the 'Bambi Syndromers'. I have discovered that the majority of the Bambis are just slogan mouthers. Their attitudes have been taken off the shelf – oven-ready and pre-packed. This saves them the trouble of thinking – thinking can damage your prejudices.

In a restaurant one evening, a 'caring' (her own description) woman took me to task for being nasty to God's creatures. She then ordered lobster. I felt it incumbent upon me to point out that that lobster was going to be boiled alive for her pleasure. At this she flew into a rage and said that that had nothing to do with anything and that I was ★★★★. To be fair to her, she then ordered a steak instead. I felt I had to point out that, by her terms, she was still an accessory to murder and she said ★★★★ to me.

In case you are interested, there is a humane way of despatching a lobster before boiling which I have on the authority of a very eminent chef: take a sharp knife, hold the lobster down with one hand, count down to 'the third bendy section', insert knife and 'wiggle it about severely'. This severs something vital – now go boil your lobster.

Woman No 2 also gave me a rollocking about my bloodstained life style. Then, as the Australian Chardonnay began to grip a bit, she told me how, each morning, she would go and inspect her slug trap and then drown the victims in a bucket of water. She had an even more fetching way with snails. She threw them up onto a bit of flat roof (she liked to hear the shells crack, she said), then she would watch the local pigeons (I did not know that pigeons ate snails, but perhaps London pigeons do) come and gobble up the living, but defenceless, creatures. I asked her if she would have done the same if the snails were small and furry with big eyes? She had the grace to admit that her attitudes were somewhat inconsistent, but said that I was still a cruel, red-faced bastard!

Hypocrisy can also be cynical. Like the newspaper editor whom I quizzed about slagging off hunting on page X and sponsoring a fishing competition on page Y. If one was 'cruel', then why not the other? 'Fishing,' he said, 'is working class, like my readers.'

[10]

'Are ye ganning to the hoonds today?' they said.

'Not I, Braw Lads,' said I, 'not I – too much work to do.'

'Man, ye carl that work, sitting in a chair, puffing yer pipe and tapping away at yon machine? Man, yon's nae work, yon's luxury.' That is certainly a point of view and one that I would have heartily endorsed when I was 'at the hoonds' the other afternoon. The south-easterly gale was driving the sleet horizontally into my face, hounds had disappeared into the deeps of the flow (pronounced like plough and = morass), where I was certainly not going to venture. The conical shape of the Black Stitchell was looming out of the scudding cloud wrack. It was dreich, drear and desolate and how I longed for my cosy office. Today was different – a light westerly wind, fleecy clouds and patches of blue sky – just the day to go to the hounds. But no – stern duty called: it was time to put another shovel of coal in the fire box of the word processor and to get to work.

I was tapping away when there came a faint, but growing sound. Could it? was it? it was!! I leaped from my chair, scattering papers, pens, pencils and a glass of water and there were hounds screaming past the office window and the huntsman jumping the fence into the field below the house. Bother the work! I was out and gone; into the wellies and the old coat and onto the faithful quadricycle that was pawing and snorting with impatience in the yard.

Hounds were over the burn and flying up the hill beyond, with the mounted field thundering behind. I waved that I would shut the gate by the bridge. Then I leant on it and watched them disappear. Something was tugging at my coat tails. That wretched little Work Ethic that I thought that I had shut firmly in the office was perched on the quad with its arms folded in a disapproving manner and a mean, tight-lipped expression. It was no good. With my tail between my legs, I went back to the office and stoked up the word processor. With a smug expression on its face, Work Ethic settled itself comfortably on a pile of box files and went to sleep.

[11]

Today the world is white. The view from the office window shows a uniform white blanket, splattered with black copses and criss-crossed with the dark lines of fences. The hills across the valley have disappeared as yet another snow storm sweeps in from the North Sea: from the Urals with love and why can they not keep the wretched stuff?

It is a picture postcard scene and that is the best place for it. As far as your average countryman (The Man on the Glanton Tractor) is concerned, snow is a 'right b****r'. It makes everything two or three times the work. The big doors on the shed have to be dug out before they can be opened to let the tractor out. The tractor will undoubtedly have 'taken the strunts' (sulking) and be unwilling to leave its warm byre. The engine makes sluggish noises, but if you are lucky it will catch on the last gasp of the failing battery.

Snow is one of the few things that can defeat the rugged quadricycle; its 4-wheel drive is of no avail if the machine becomes completely 'foondered' and where is the spade that is supposed to live on the rear carrier? Inevitably it has been 'borrowed' by person, or persons, unknown and you are going to have to trudge back to the steading to find it.

By this time the hungry cows are yelling for their breakfast and your own is receding over the psychological horizon.

The sheep are all clustered around the gates, waiting for their own meals-on-wheels service. You meant to turn the feed troughs over last night, but forgot, so they have to be emptied of snow, before the feed can be put in. The collies have to keep the ewes back. There is nothing funny about being knocked bustle over apex by a horde of ravening mule yowes, maddened by the rustle of a feed sack. The hay hecks (racks) have to be filled. You have to take your gloves off to get your knife out to cut the strings on the bales, then you sharp (sic) find out why Shakespeare's Dick the Shepherd 'blows his nail'; blowing on your thumbnail brings a little warmth to frozen hands.

The ice on the water troughs has to be broken (sometimes with a lump hammer) and the shards removed with the bare hands. It is a lovesome thing to get the gloves on again.

The farm road is blocked. All the gates are snowed in and we shall see neither butcher nor baker and certainly not the candlestick maker until things 'take up a bit'. This is why we have two 4×4 vehicles. There are almost as many 4×4s in this part of the world as there are in Central London which so often gets blocked by blizzards.

All in all, the stockman's morning round can take a very long time in the snow and he is mightily relieved to chug back into the yard with snow-encrusted dogs chasing each other round and round; they seem to enjoy the snow. But soft! what is this entrancing thing? this tendril of scent that sets the nose whiffling and the taste buds salivating? It is the smell of frying bacon wafting across the yard, bringing with it visions of eggs and sausages and mugs of steaming tea and the after-breakfast pipe and warm feet: then you can say: 'B****R the snow!'

Talking of breakfasts, the Memsahib and I have Brunch on a Sunday every now and again, especially when the winter mornings are so dark. The last one we had was a truly memorable meal because it was an amalgam of dimly remembered yet almost forgotten tastes and flavours. This was a breakfast as breakfasts used to be. There were fried goose eggs and I do not suppose that many of you have ever eaten one (you would do well to eat two – a goose egg fills a plate). They were fresh eggs, too. Just the sight of that firm white and the great golden yolk in the middle made me salivate, but the explosion of flavour in the mouth! and, yes, I know that you have forgotten that eggs can actually taste of anything. As your 'Farm Fresh' supermarket eggs probably came from a Polish battery farm six weeks ago, I am not surprised.

With eggs there must be bacon. I had given up English bacon as a bad job. But this day we had two sorts of Gloucester Old Spot bacon from the great Mr Lutwych (*see* Appendix). The GOP is a Rare Breed. It is a slow-maturing pig and has a bit of fat about it, so, no good for Supermarket Woman. But without fat and without proper hanging there can be no flavour and I have not tasted flavour like that since I was a tacker. And think on this – the more GOPs you eat, the sooner they will cease to be a Rare Breed.

Of course, there must be sausages especially on cold winter mornings. We had two sorts of GOP sausage and a venison sausage from the great Mr Green of Longframlington. And you need black pudding to sop up all that lovely rich egg yolk – especially you need that wonderful crisp spicy pudding from the Higginsons (*see* Appendix, chapter 5). After a brunch like that the only thing to do is to slacken the belt, pour another cup of tea, light the pipe, close your eyes and think of *flavour*.

[12]

Kind people keep telling me that we have had a terrible winter 'in the north'. I have to tell them that this is not the case and that it has been an extremely clement winter in Northumberland. Of course one has to realise that 'north' for many people means north of Potters Bar (wherever that is). I am always slightly bemused at the metropolitan inability to grasp the scale of distances. I remember an editor suggesting that I 'pop along to Doncaster for me; it must be near you'. Doncaster is almost exactly halfway between here and London and means three hours' fast driving.

Doncaster may well have had a terrible winter, but we have not. Mind you, there have been days when 4-wheel drive has come in handy which brings me to a rather sad little story. I have often wondered at the number of Range-Rovers in London and what can be the use of them. It was snowing lightly on the M62 and the traffic policeman came upon a Range-Rover, stationary in the middle lane, from which a woman was decanting herself and her luggage. She explained that she was from Hayes (Middx.) and was abandoning her vehicle because of the snow (about half an inch). 'But madam,' says the copper, 'you won't get stuck in that – it's got 4-wheel drive.' 'What,' said the woman, 'is 4-wheel drive?'

Bad weather in the hills is not to be taken lightly – it can kill. Even experienced hill men can get caught out. People here still remember the sudden November blizzard in which two hill shepherds perished, one of them within 100 yards of his steading, although the poor man probably did not realise this in the white-out conditions. A shepherd's wife told me of the time her husband staggered in out of the snow and she had to chip the ice off his coat before she could unbutton it. He was far too stiff to do it – he only just made it.

I spend a great deal of time alone in high, wild places where the weather can turn on you with the speed of an enraged wife. I am always warmly clad in layers of clothing and wonderful boots but, were I to be injured in acres of precipitous sitka spruce, or on a rock-strewn hillside, I would take a deal of finding, especially in my camouflaged clothing. I always carry a survival blanket (any good outdoor shop) in my hip pocket, a bar of chocolate, a whistle and a small strobe light flasher.

A tip that I have not yet tried – a certain Scottish newspaper, with stranded motorists in mind, recommended filling condoms with urine and using them as hot water bottles in an emergency.

This idea does seem to beg several questions of ways and means, but it might come in handy when your Range-Rover is snowbound in Curzon Street.

[13]

I am grounded with cracked ribs. The lay-off has coincided with a spell of the most lovely gentle winter weather which gave added pleasure to all country pursuits, so my fettle has been rendered definitely tatty by inaction. But all has not been lost. I managed to add a couple of does to the cull, in spite of the fact that walking has been difficult and crawling and climbing definitely out. We managed by the simple expedient of Fred driving me out into the woods, propping me up against a tree and disappearing for a couple of hours, until the winter dusk had turned truly black. It was just a question of patience and stillness. One evening a rabbit appeared and sat cleaning his whiskers within a foot of my boots. On another occasion, a big dog fox passed me so close that I could have prodded him with my stick. It is these sort of silly little things that give me so much pleasure even if I never see a deer.

The other evening I sat and watched two does feeding for nearly two hours, until the dark enveloped them. I could not move and they never offered the chance of a safe shot, but I enjoyed watching them.

[14]

There was a group of us out on the hill yesterday. We were surrounded by a hanging blanket of fog into which hounds had long since disappeared from sight and, more recently, from hearing: they might have disappeared from the face of the earth – or over the Border fence and into Scotland, which is pretty much the same thing. The best thing to do seemed to be to have a cup of tea and 'a bit crack' (polished and amusing conversation). As is so often the case on these occasions, the conversation ranged over various fascinating topics, but with a solid foundation of sheep, the ailments of sheep and lubricious gossip.

For instance, the company was convinced that the purpose of the ladder (from which I had fallen to break the ribs that I was nursing) was to enable me to look through the bedroom window of a local widow lady of impeccable virtue. The company rejoiced accordingly. We then passed on to other subjects, such as the efficacy of urine as an emergency antiseptic. This reminded me of a formidable lady in Devon whose temperament was rendered seriously uneven by her old father's deafness. As last she dragged him off to see the new young doctor (recently of Welwyn, Herts). The lady explained to the doctor that she had come about 'Father's yearin' ', whereupon the young man presented her with a specimen bottle and suitable instructions.

'You silly born bugger,' said the lady, ' 'tis nothing wrong with 'is water; 'tis 'is yearin'. 'ee'm so deaf as a bliddy post.' I do think it rather a nonsense that people in this country are being exhorted to learn French and German when many of them have not even been taught to speak Devon proper (sic).

[15]

It was late in the afternoon when hounds were drawing up the Bloody Cleugh, a steep little ravine full of birch and scrub oak. A party of us had stopped our quadricycles on the edge of the Cleugh to watch and listen. It was a still evening with a frosty sun dropping towards the western horizon. As we sat, we heard this strange churring noise:

'Pigeons,' someone suggested. Then someone else pointed out a large black shape perched in a tree across the ravine: 'Yon's blackcock.' Then the whole pack exploded out of the wood, a splendid sight. They were male black grouse and we counted at least fifteen. Someone said that they had not seen such a number 'these many years' and someone else said that they had never seen them roosting in trees before. The black grouse is certainly a bird of the open moorland, but I suppose that there is no reason why they should not roost in trees when such things are available. It is certainly good security. Anyway it does not matter. It was certainly good to see a pack like that.

And so tired men, tired hounds and tired horses rode away in the gathering gloom and hardening frost.

[16]

'When one door closes, another opens' is what they say.

The end of March sees the end of the hunting season in the Northumbrian hills, more or less. Some packs will go on a bit into April, but as most of the people concerned have lambing starting or imminent, the hunting tends to grind to a halt. There is no tradition on this side of the country of 'lambing calls' such as they have in the Lake District. There, if a fox is taking lambs, the farmer telephones the hunt and the huntsman appears at dawn the next morning with a few tried and trusted old hounds. The idea is to hit off the overnight drag of the marauder from the edge of the lambing field and hunt him to destruction. I say 'him', but it is often 'her'. The worst lamb killers are often 'yeld' (barren) vixens or vixens whose cubs have been destroyed.

Conversely, a lot of old shepherds will tell you that the best thing is to have a vixen with cubs hard by your lambing field. A vixen never kills on her own doorstep and will discourage others from so doing. When I farmed in Yorkshire, I had a block of fields on the edge of the forestry where trouble might have been expected. Every year a vixen reared her cubs in a bank on the land and I never lost a lamb to foxes. Back in Northumberland, the shepherds expect the hounds to have killed enough foxes before the lambing to prevent them having trouble.

It is always sad to see the end of another hunting season, but we do start in August and by the end of March (and c. 100 days' hunting) things are getting a bit stale. There are heavy, and indeed milking, vixens about who should not be disturbed. It is generally time to finish.

In March one hopes for a few nice days and perhaps a small *bonne bouche* of spring. Days when one can sit on the hill in the sun, watching hounds and saying to the neighbour: 'Not much of a hunting day, mind, but Man, it's grand to feel the sun on your back'. There have been some nice days, but more often: 'Aye, it would be grand day, but for the bloody wind.' Like the other day (windy, but a lovely sunny day) when hounds found a fox and ran up, up, up and over the Border at the 'Scotch Fence'. I was bumbling on behind, bumping in and out of some ghastly peat haggs – the quad had already 'cowped' with me once – when suddenly in came a wicked storm. It was a complete white-out of hard, driving snow coming horizontally all the way from Greenland. There was nothing to do but batten down, feel miserable and wonder whether my nose was really as broken as it felt.

And, finally . . .

We were all very sorry when Jim's old Border Terrier died. We had a bit of a wake for the dog, after which Jim weaved home to bury it.

We were also very sorry when Jim broke a leg on the fell and was laid up. Him being a bachelor, all the neighbours rallied round to see that he did not lack. George called in one day to see if there was owt that he could do to help. Jim said that yes, there was something; if George could get a few tatties out of the sack that was under the sink in the back kitchen and peel them, then Jim could hobble through later and put them on the boil. George returned bravish sharp to report that the only thing in a sack under the sink was the corpse of a Border Terrier, well past its sell-by date.

'Hooshyerbugger!' cried Jim. 'I doot but I've buried the tatties!'

APPENDIX

Chapter 2

ARTICLE 2: *Memories of Strathvaich*, the memoirs of Kenneth Mac-Lennan, the head stalker. This is now out of print but try Grayling Books on 01931 715282.

ARTICLE 4: 'Willy Poole's Reel' can be heard in the talking books version of *The Backwoodsman's Year* available from Soundings, King's Drive, Whitley Bay, Northumberland NE26 5JT. Tel. 01912 534155.

ARTICLE 7: for Robert Allen's tape, telephone 01434 220265.

Chapter 5

ARTICLE 2: Beauchamp's Restaurant and Fish Shop in Leadenhall Market: Tel. 0171 621 1362.

ARTICLE 3: The Black Pudding finalists were:
Higginsons Ltd of Main Street, Grange-over-Sands, Cumbria.
Husband & Wife Ltd, Stall 30, Pontypridd Market, Glamorgan.
Thorney Ltd of Ridgewood Road, Chorley, Lancashire.

ARTICLE 4: For some of the best kippers in the world (available mail order) contact John Swallow of Swallow Fish Ltd, 2 South Street, Seahouses, Northumberland. Tel. 01665 721052.

ARTICLE 7: For a copy of the booklet *Scotch Whisky – questions and answers* contact The Scotch Whisky Association, 20 Atholl Crescent, Edinburgh EH3 8HF. Tel. 0131 222 9200.

Chapter 8

ARTICLE 8: For your own Yo! Heave! Ho!, telephone Captain Lapthorne on 01752 872616.

Chapter 9

ARTICLE 4: Ian Alcock (wildlife writer, especially deer) and his wife Diana E. Brown (wildlife artist) may be contacted on 013398 84207.

Chapter 12

ARTICLE 6: There is no edition of *The Fox's Prophecy* in print at the time of writing, but you might find the version with my commentary from Grayling Books, tel. 01931 715282.

ARTICLE 11: For the best bacon I have tasted in a long time, I went to Richard Lutwych, The Cotswold Gourmet in Cirencester, who specialises in meat from rare breeds. Tel. 01285 860229.

INDEX